AMERICAN SLAVES TELL THEIR STORIES

SIX INTERVIEWS

Mrs. Octavia V. R. Albert.

AMERICAN SLAVES TELL THEIR STORIES
SIX INTERVIEWS

Octavia V. Rogers Albert

Introduction by
Willard F. Mallalieu

DOVER PUBLICATIONS, INC.
Mineola, New York

Bibliographical Note

This Dover edition, first published in 2005, is a newly reset, unabridged republication of the work originally published by Hunt & Eaton, New York, and Cranston & Stowe, Cincinnati, in 1890 under the title *The House of Bondage, or Charlotte Brooks and Other Slaves.*

Library of Congress Cataloging-in-Publication Data

Albert, Octavia V. Rogers (Octavia Victoria Rogers), 1853–1889?
[House of bondage, or, Charlotte Brooks and other slaves]
American slaves tell their stories : six interviews / Octavia V. Rogers Albert; introduction by Willard F. Mallalieu.
p. cm.
Originally published: The house of bondage, or, Charlotte Brooks and other slaves. New York: Hunt & Eaton, 1890.
ISBN 0-486-44190-3 (pbk.)
1. Slaves—Southern States—Interviews. 2. Women slaves—Southern States—Interviews. 3. Slaves—Southern States—Social conditions—19th century. I. Title.

E444.A33 2005
306.3'092275—dc22

2004061895

Manufactured in the United States of America
Dover Publications, Inc., 31 East 2nd Street, Mineola, N.Y. 11501

THE HOUSE OF BONDAGE

OR

CHARLOTTE BROOKS AND OTHER SLAVES

ORIGINAL AND LIFE-LIKE, AS THEY APPEARED IN THEIR
OLD PLANTATION AND CITY SLAVE LIFE; TOGETHER
WITH PEN-PICTURES OF THE PECULIAR INSTI-
TUTION, WITH SIGHTS AND INSIGHTS
INTO THEIR NEW RELATIONS
AS FREEDMEN, FREEMEN,
AND CITIZENS

BY

MRS. OCTAVIA V. ROGERS ALBERT

WITH AN INTRODUCTION

BY

REV. BISHOP WILLARD F. MALLALIEU, D.D.

NEW YORK: HUNT & EATON
CINCINNATI: CRANSTON & STOWE
1890

[Original title page]

PREFACE

THE following pages, giving the result of conversations and other information gathered, digested, and written by Mrs. Octavia V. Rogers, deceased wife of the Rev. A. E. P. Albert, A.M., D.D., first appeared in the columns of the *South-western Christian Advocate,* some months after her death, as a serial story, under the name of *The House of Bondage.* It was received with such enthusiasm and appreciation that no sooner was the story concluded than letters poured in upon the editor from all directions, urging him to put it in book form, so as to preserve it as a memorial of the author, as well as for its intrinsic value as a history of negro slavery in the Southern States, of its overthrow, and of the mighty and far-reaching results derived therefrom.

No special literary merit is claimed for the work. No special effort was made in that direction; but as a panoramic exhibition of slave-life, emancipation, and the subsequent results, the story herein given, with all the facts brought out, as each one speaks for himself and in his own way, is most interesting and life-like.

The conversations herein given are not imaginary, but actual, and given as they actually occurred. No one can read these pages without realizing the fact that "truth is often stranger than fiction." As such we present it to the public as an unpretentious contribution to an epoch in American history that will more and more rivet the attention of the civilized world as the years roll around.

An only daughter unites with the writer in sending out these pages penned by a precious and devoted mother and wife, whose angelic spirit is constantly seen herein, and whose subtle and holy influence seems to continue to guide and protect both in the path over which they since have had to travel without the presence and cheer of her inspiring countenance.

To her sacred memory these pages, the result of her efforts, are affectionately inscribed.

A. E. P. ALBERT
LAURA T. F. ALBERT

EDITORIAL ROOMS
South-western Christian Advocate,
NEW ORLEANS, LA., *November* 15, 1890.

CONTENTS

xi

INTRODUCTION

THE story of slavery never has been and never will be fully told. In the last letter that John Wesley ever wrote, addressed to Wilberforce, the great abolitionist, and dated February 24, 1791, and this only six days before his tireless hand was quieted in death, he wrote these words: "I see not how you can go through your glorious enterprise in opposing that execrable villainy" (slavery and the slave-trade), "which is the scandal of religion, of England, and of human nature. Unless God has raised you up for this very thing you will be worn out by the opposition of men and devils; but if God be for you who can be against you? Are all of them together stronger than God? O, 'be not weary in well doing.' Go on in the name of God and the power of his might till even American slavery, the vilest that ever saw the sun, shall vanish away before it."

It is because American slavery was "the vilest that ever saw the sun" that it is and will remain forever impossible to adequately portray its unspeakable horrors, its heartbreaking sorrows, its fathomless miseries of hopeless grief, its intolerable shames, and its heaven-defying and outrageous brutalities.

But while it remains true that the story can never be completely told, it is wise and well that the task should be attempted and in part performed; and this for the reason that there are some who presume that this slavery, "the vilest that ever saw the sun," has been, and is still, of divine appointment; in short, that from first to last it was a divine institution. It is well to remind all such people that the Almighty Ruler of the universe is not an accessory, either before or after the fact, to such crimes as were involved in slavery. Let no guilty man, let no descendant of such man, attempt to excuse the sin and shame of slave-holding on the ground of its providential character. The truth is that slavery is the product of human greed and lust and oppression, and not of God's ordering.

Then it is well to write about slavery that the American people may know from what depths of disgrace and infamy they rose when, guided by the hand of God, they broke every yoke and let the oppressed go free. Finally, it is well to tell, though only in part, the story of slavery so that every man, woman, and child of the once enslaved race may know the exceeding mercy of God that has delivered them from the hopeless and helpless despair that might have been their portion if the Lord God Omnipotent had not come forth to smite in divine and righteous wrath the proud oppressor and bring his long-suffering people out of their worse than Egyptian bondage.

This volume, penned by a hand that now rests in the quiet of the tomb, is a contribution to the sum total of the story that can never be entirely told.

In her young girlhood the author had known the accursed system, and she knew the joy of deliverance. With a deep, pathetic tenderness she loved her race; she would gladly have died for their enlightenment and salvation. But she has gone to her reward, leaving behind her the precious legacy of a sweet Christian influence that can only flow forth from a pure and consecrated life.

May this volume go forth to cheer and comfort and inspire to high and holy deeds all who shall read its pages!

WILLARD F. MALLALIEU

BOSTON, MASS., *Nov.* 15, 1890.

THE AUTHOR

THE author of this volume, Octavia Victoria Rogers, wife of the Rev. A. E. P. Albert, D.D., was born in Oglethorpe, Macon County, Ga., of slave parentage, December 24, 1853, and was educated at Atlanta University, in that State. She and Dr. Albert first met at Montezuma, Ga., where they taught school together, in 1873; and on October 21, 1874, they were united in holy wedlock. They had an only daughter, who survives her mother. She united with the African Methodist Episcopal Church under the preaching of Bishop H. M. Turner, at Oglethorpe, Ga., and was converted and united with the Methodist Episcopal Church, under the pastorate of the Rev. Marcus Dole, at Union Chapel, New Orleans, in 1875. Her own husband baptized her at Houma, La., in 1878, during the first year of his ministry. She was an angel of mercy whose loving spirit will long be cherished by all who knew her but to love her. Now she rests from her labors, and her good works do follow her. Peace to her precious memory!

COMPILER

CHAPTER I

CHARLOTTE BROOKS

Causes of immorality among colored people—Charlotte Brooks—She
is sold South—Sunday work.

NONE but those who resided in the South during the time of
slavery can realize the terrible punishments that were visited upon the slaves. Virtue and self-respect were denied them.

Much has been written concerning the negro, and we must
confess that the moral standing of the race is far from what it
should be; but who is responsible for the sadly immoral condition of this illiterate race in the South? I answer unhesitatingly,
Their masters.

Consider that here in this Bible land, where we have the light,
where the Gospel was preached Sunday after Sunday in all portions of the South, and where ministers read from the pulpit
that God had made of one blood all nations of men, etc., that
nevertheless, with the knowledge and teachings of the word of
God, the slaves were reduced to a level with the brute. The half
was never told concerning this race that was in bondage nearly
two hundred and fifty years.

The great judgment-day is before us; "for we must all appear
before the judgment-seat of Christ." There are millions of souls
now crowned around the throne of God who have washed their
robes white and are praising God, although they spent their lives
in sorrow, but who will rise up in judgment and condemn this
Christian nation. The Spanish Inquisition can hardly compare
with the punishments visited upon this once enslaved race. But
let me introduce you to some characters that will amply illus-
trate what I mean.

It was in the fall of 1879 that I met Charlotte Brooks. She was

1

brought from the State of Virginia and sold in the State of Louisiana many years before the war. I have spent hours with her listening to her telling of her sad life of bondage in the cane-fields of Louisiana. She was always willing to speak of "old master and mistress." I remember one morning as she entered my home I said to her, "Good-morning, Aunt Charlotte; how are you feeling to-day?"

She said, "La, my child, I didn't sleep hardly last night; my poor old bones ached me so bad I could not move my hand for a while."

"What's the cause of it?"

"Why, old marster used to make me go out before day, in high grass and heavy dews, and I caught cold. I lost all of my health. I tell you, nobody knows the trouble I have seen. I have been sold three times. I had a little baby when my second marster sold me, and my last old marster would make me leave my child before day to go to the cane-field; and he would not allow me to come back till ten o'clock in the morning to nurse my child. When I did go I could hear my poor child crying long before I got to it. And la, me! my poor child would be so hungry when I'd get to it! Sometimes I would have to walk more than a mile to get to my child, and when I did get there I would be so tired I'd fall asleep while my baby was sucking. He did not allow me much time to stay with my baby when I did go to nurse it. Sometimes I would overstay my time with my baby; then I would have to run all the way back to the field. O, I tell you nobody knows the trouble we poor colored folks had to go through with here in Louisiana. I had heard people say Louisiana was a hard place for black people, and I didn't want to come; but old marster took me and sold me from my mother anyhow, and from my sisters and brothers in Virginia.

"I have never seen or heard from them since I left old Virginia. That's been more than thirty-five years ago. When I left old Virginia my mother cried for me, and when I saw my poor mother with tears in her eyes I thought I would die. O, it was a sad day for me when I was to leave my mother in old Virginia. My mother used to take her children to church every Sunday. But when I came to Louisiana I did not go to church any more.

Every body was Catholic where I lived, and I had never seen that sort of religion that has people praying on beads. That was all strange to me. The older I got the more I thought of my mother's Virginia religion. Sometimes when I was away off in the cane-field at work it seemed I could hear my mother singing the 'Old Ship of Zion.' I could never hear any of the old Virginia hymns sung here, for every body was Catholic around where I stayed."

"Aunt Charlotte, did you say you *never* attended church any more after leaving Virginia?"

"No, my child; I never saw inside of a church after I came to Louisiana."

"What did you do on the Sabbath?"

"La, me! I had plenty to do. Old mistress would make me help in the kitchen on Sundays when I had nothing else to do. Mistress was Catholic, and her church was a good ways off, and she did not go often to church. In rolling season we all worked Sunday and Monday grinding cane. Old marster did not care for Sunday; he made all of us work hard on Sunday as well as any other day when he was pushed up. 'Most all the planters worked on Sunday in rolling season where I lived. In Virginia every body rested and would go to church on Sunday, and it was strange to see every body working on Sunday here. O, how I used to wish to hear some of the old Virginia hymns!

"I remember my mother used to have a minister to come to see her in Virginia, and he would read the Bible and sing. He used to sing, 'O where are the Hebrew children? Safe in the promised land.' I did not have religion when I came out here. I did not have any body to tell me any thing about repentance, but I always prayed, and the more I would pray the better I would feel. I never would fail to say my prayers, and I just thought if I could get back to my old Virginia home to hear some of my mother's old-time praises it would do my soul good. But, poor me! I could never go back to my old Virginia home."

CHAPTER II

CHARLOTTE'S STORY

Meeting Jane Lee from Virginia—Conversion of Charlotte Brooks.

"FOUR years after I came to Louisiana the speculators brought another woman out here from my old State. She was sold to a man near my marster's plantation. I heard of it, and, thinks I, 'That might be some of my kinsfolks, or somebody that knew my mother.' So the first time I got a chance I went to see the woman. My white folks did not want the 'niggers' to go off on Sundays; but anyhow my old marster let me go sometimes after dinner on Sunday evenings. So I went to see who the woman was, and I tell you, my child, when I got in the road going I could not go fast enough, for it just seemed to me that the woman was one of my folks. I walked a while and would run a while. By and by I got there. As I went in the gate I met a man, and I asked him what was the woman's name; he said her name was Jane Lee. I went around to the quarters where all the black people lived, and I found her. I went up to her and said, 'Howdy do, Aunt Jane?' She said, 'How do you know me, child?' I said, 'I heard you just came from Virginia; I came from that State too. I just been out here four years. I am so glad to see you, Aunt Jane. Where did you come from in Virginia?' 'I came from Richmond. I have left all of my people in Virginia.'

"Aunt Jane was no kin to me, but I felt that she was because she came from my old home. Me and Aunt Jane talked and cried that Sunday evening till nearly dark. Aunt Jane said she left her children, and it almost killed her to ever think of them. She said one was only five years old. Her old marster got in debt, and he sold her to pay his debts. I told her I had left all of my people too, and that I was a poor lone creature to myself when I first

4

came out from Virginia. Aunt Jane asked me did the people have churches here. I told her no; that I had not been in a church since I came here. She had religion, and she was as good a woman as you ever saw. She could read the Bible, and could sing so many pretty hymns. Aunt Jane said it seemed to her she was lost because she could not go to church and hear preaching and singing like she used to hear in Virginia. She said people didn't care for Sunday in Louisiana."

"Aunt Charlotte, it must have been a joyful time with you when you first saw Aunt Jane Lee."

"Yes, I tell you. I stayed with her till evening. I was afraid old marster would not let me go to see Aunt Jane any more, and when I got in the road, I tell you I did not lose any time. It was dark when I left Aunt Jane; but before I left her house she prayed and sang, and it made me feel glad to hear her pray and sing. It made me think of my old Virginia home and my mother. She sang,

> "'Guide me, O thou great Jehovah,
> Pilgrim through this barren land.'

"I had heard that hymn before, but had forgot it. All next week it seemed to me I could hear the old Virginia hymn Aunt Jane sung for me that Sunday evening when I was working in the cane-field.

"It was nearly rolling season when Aunt Jane first came to Louisiana, and we all was so busy working night and day I did not have a chance to see her in a long time after I left her that Sunday evening. But two or three months after that I got a chance to go to see her again. Old marster let me go and stay all day that Sunday. He said we all had made such a good year's work, and he was mighty well pleased with us. But he was not always glad and pleased with us. Sometimes he would get mad about something going wrong on the place, and he would beat every one of us and lock us up in the jail he made for us."

"What! Did he put you in jail on Sunday?"

"Yes; 'most every Sunday morning when we did not have any work to do. The next time I went to see Aunt Jane we had another happy time. She could read right good in the Bible and hymn-book, and she would read to me one or two hymns at a time. I remember she read to me about Daniel in the lions' den, and about the king having the three Hebrew children cast in the fiery furnace, and when he looked in the flames of fire he saw four men, and one looked like the Son of God. O, how Aunt Jane used to love to read about the Hebrew children!

"I finally got religion, and it was Aunt Jane's praying and singing them old Virginia hymns that helped me so much. Aunt Jane's marster would let her come to see me sometimes, but not often. Sometimes she would slip away from her place at night and come to see me anyhow. She would hold prayer-meeting in my house whenever she would come to see me."

"Would your marster allow you to hold prayer-meeting on his place?"

"No, my child; if old marster heard us singing and praying he would come out and make us stop. One time, I remember, we all were having a prayer-meeting in my cabin, and marster came up to the door and hollered out, 'You, *Charlotte,* what's all that fuss in there?' We all had to hush up for that night. I was so afraid old marster would see Aunt Jane. I knew Aunt Jane would have to suffer if her white people knew she was off at night. Marster used to say God was tired of us all hollering to him at night."

"Did any of the black people on his place believe in the teachings of their master?"

"No, my child; none of us listened to him about singing and praying. I tell you we used to have some good times together praying and singing. He did not want us to pray, but we would have our little prayer-meeting anyhow. Sometimes when we met to hold our meetings we would put a big wash-tub full of water in the middle of the floor to catch the sound of our voices when we sung. When we all sung we would march around and shake each other's hands, and we would sing easy and low, so marster could not hear us. O, how happy I used to be in those meetings, although I was a slave! I thank the Lord Aunt Jane Lee lived by me. She helped me to make my peace with the Lord. O, the day I was converted! It seemed to me it was a paradise here below!

It looked like I wanted nothing any more. Jesus was so sweet to my soul! Aunt Jane used to sing, 'Jesus! the name that charms our fears.' That hymn just suited my case. Sometimes I felt like preaching myself. It seemed I wanted to ask every body if they loved Jesus when I first got converted. I wanted to ask old marster, but he was Creole, and did not understand what I said much. Aunt Jane was the cause of so many on our plantation getting religion. We did not have any church to go to, but she would talk to us about old Virginia, how people done there. She said them beads and crosses we saw every body have was nothing. She said people must give their hearts to God, to love him and keep his commandments; and we believed what she said. I never wanted them beads I saw others have, for I just thought we would pray without any thing, and that God only wanted the heart."

CHAPTER III

AUNT CHARLOTTE'S FRIENDS

Death of Aunt Charlotte's children—Jane Lee's master leaves the neighborhood—Nellie Johnson tries to escape to her old Virginia home.

"AUNT Charlotte, what became of your baby? were you blest to raise it?"

"No; my poor child died when it was two years old. Old marster's son was the father of my child."

"Did its father help to take care of it?"

"Why, no; he never noticed my child."

"Did you have any more children?"

"Yes; but they all died."

"Why could you not rear any of them?"

"La, me, child! they died for want of attention. I used to leave them alone half of the time. Sometimes old mistress would have some one to mind them till they got so they could walk, but after that they would have to paddle for themselves. I was glad the Lord took them, for I knowed they were better off with my blessed Jesus than with me."

Poor Charlotte Brooks! I can never forget how her eyes were filled with tears when she would speak of all her children: "Gone, and no one to care for me!" Sometimes she failed to come and see me (for she always visited me when she was able; never missed a day, unless she was sick, during the two years I lived near her). She was in poor health, and had no one to help her in her old age, when she really needed help. She had spent her life working hard for her masters, and after giving all of her youthful days to them was turned upon this cold, unfriendly world with nothing. She left her master's plantation with two

8

blankets, and was several days on the road walking to get to the town of ——, and, having become so exhausted, dropped them by the way-side. She said when she arrived at her destination she had nothing but the clothes she had on her back. She was then old and feeble.

I remember she used to come and beg me to save the stale coffee for her, saying she had not eaten any thing all day. Notwithstanding all of her poverty she was always rejoicing in the love of God. I asked her once whether she felt lonely in this unfriendly world.

She answered, "No, my dear; how can a child of God feel lonesome? My heavenly Father took care of me in slave-time. He led me all the way along, and now he has set me free, and I am free both in soul and body."

She said, "I heard a preacher say once since I got free, 'Not a foot of land do I possess, not a cottage in the wilderness.' Just so it is with me; sometimes I don't have bread to eat; but I tell you, my soul is always feasting on my dear Jesus. Nobody knows what it is to taste of Jesus but them that has been washed by him. Many years ago, my white folks did not want me even to pray, and would whip me for praying, saying it was foolishness for me to pray. But the more old marster whipped me the more I'd pray. Sometimes he'd put me in jail; but, la, me! it did not stop me from praying. I'd kneel down on the jail floor and pray often, and nearly all day Sundays. I'd fall asleep sometimes praying. Old marster would come and call me about sundown. He would always call out loud before he got to the jail to let me know he was coming. I could always tell his walk. I tell you, I used to feel rested and good when he let me out. He let me go so I could always be ready to go to work on Monday morning. One Sunday night, just as I got to my door, Aunt Jane met me. I was just coming from the jail, too. I knowed Aunt Jane was coming to hold prayer-meeting, and I hurried. If old marster heard us he would put me in jail the next Sunday morning; but, child, that did not stop me; I was always ready for the prayer-meeting. I told Aunt Jane I had been in jail all day, and it was a happy day in jail, too.

"Aunt Jane's white folks was not so hard on her as mine was. They did not let her go off at night, but she would slip away and come and lead prayer-meeting at my house. She always brought her Bible and hymn-book. She read to us that night something like this: 'I know my Redeemer lives.'"

I said to her, "O, yes, Aunt Charlotte; I remember it very well. It is in the book of Job, nineteenth chapter, twenty-fifth verse."

"Well, it has been so long since I heard it read. Wont you get the Bible and please read it for me?"

"With much pleasure I'll read it to you. Here it is: 'For I know that my Redeemer liveth, and that he shall stand at the latter day upon the earth: and though after my skin worms destroy this body, yet in my flesh shall I see God: whom I shall see for myself, and mine eyes shall behold, and not another; though my reins be consumed within me.' I've read three verses of that chapter for you."

"Thank you, too, for it. O, how it makes me think of them happy times in the cane-field I used to have! I do wish I could read. I long to read the Bible and hymn-book. When I was in Virginia I used to study some. I learned my A, B, C, and begun to spell some in my blue-back spelling-book. I could spell 'ba-ker' and 'sha-dy,' and all along there in the spelling-book; but after I came to Louisiana I forgot every thing."

I said, "You have no hope of learning, now that you are free, although you are at liberty to do as you please?"

"No, my child; I can't see how to thread my needle now. I have given all my young days to the white folks. My eye-sight is gone. Nothing for me to do but to wait till my Jesus comes."

"Aunt Charlotte, what became of Jane Lee?"

"Well, about five or six years before the war her marster moved 'way off to Texas, and I never saw her any more. We all cried when she left us. We felt lost, because we had nobody to lead us in our little meetings. After a while I begun to lead, and then some of the others would lead. Aunt Jane caused many of our people to get religion on our place. Where she lived the black folks were all Catholic, and she could not do much with them. I tell you, them Catholic people loved them beads and crosses they used to pray to. The last time Aunt Jane was with us she told us her white people was going to move, and she might never see us any more in this world; but she said, 'Charlotte, promise me you will meet me in heaven.' And then she turned around to all the others in the little cabin that night and asked them all to promise to meet her there. We all promised to fight on till death. La, me! such crying there in that little cabin that night! Aunt Jane cried, and we cried too. It was past midnight when we all parted. Aunt Jane had about two miles to go after she left our place that night. She lived about two miles from our plantation.

"Aunt Jane said that when she came out here a pretty woman was brought here with her by the name of Nellie Johnson. Nellie was sold to a mighty bad man. She tried to run away to her old Virginia home, but the white men caught her and brought her back. Aunt Jane told me Nellie was almost white, and had pretty, long, straight hair. When they got her back they made her wear men's pants for one year. They made her work in the field in that way. She said they put deer-horns on her head to punish her, with bells on them. Aunt Jane said once while she was passing on the levee she saw Nellie working with the men on the Mississippi River, and she had men's clothes on then. The white folks used to have the levee worked on often before the war. They were afraid the levees would cave in."

CHAPTER IV

CRUEL MASTERS

Nellie Johnson is barbarously treated—Sam Wilson living in the swamps of Louisiana—Richard's wife living on another plantation—His master refuses to allow him to visit her—He is caught by the patrollers and beaten almost to death.

"AUNT Jane loved Nellie, although Nellie was no kin to her, and she used to talk very often to me about her white people using her so bad. She said once that a baby was born to Nellie on the road when she was coming in the speculator's drove, and the speculator gave the child away to a white woman near by where they camped that night. The speculator said they could not take care of the child on the road, and told Nellie it was better to let the white woman have the child."

"Poor Nellie! I reckon she was trying to go back to see her child when she was caught by the white barbarous, creatures who evidently were without human nature."

"Yes, I think so too," said Aunt Charlotte, "for blood is thicker than water. The white people thought in slave-time we poor darkies had no soul, and they separated us like dogs. So many poor colored people are dead from grieving at the separation of their children that was sold away from them."

"Aunt Jane said Nellie's owner was *so* bad! She said they had a man named Sam Wilson; he stayed one half of his time in the swamp. His marster used to get after him to whip him, but Sam would not let his marster beat him. He would run off and stayed in the woods two and three months at a time. The white folks would set the dogs behind him, but Sam could not be caught by the dogs. The colored people said Sam greased his feet with rabbit-grease, and that kept the dogs from him. Aunt Jane said to me that she did not know what Sam used, but it looked like Sam could go off and stay as long as he wanted when the white folks got after him."

Aunt Charlotte said to me, "I tell you, my child, nobody could get me to run away in those Louisiana swamps. Death is but death, and I just thought if I'd run off in those swamps I'd die. I used to hear old people say it was just as well to die with fever as with ague; and that is what I thought. Aunt Jane said Sam was from Louisiana, and was a Catholic. She said she did not know what sort of religion Sam's was, to let people dance and work all day Sunday. She used to try to get Sam to come to her prayer-meetings, but she could not get him inside the door when they was praying and singing. She said Sam used to laugh at them, and call our religion ''Merican niggers' religion.'"

"Aunt Charlotte, how many of you all used to carry on prayer-meeting after Aunt Jane left?"

"Well, let me count; we had Mary, Lena, Annie, Ann, Sarah, Nancy, and Martha—seven sisters and four brethren, Billy, Green, Jones, and Richard. La, me! what a good time we all used to have in my cabin on that plantation! I think of them good, happy times we used to have now since freedom, and wish I could see all of them once more. I tell you, child, religion is good anywhere—at the plow-handle, at the hoe-handle, anywhere. If you are filled with the love of my Jesus you are happy.

Why, the best times I ever had was when I first got religion, and when old marster would put me in that old jail-house on his plantation all day Sunday.

"Richard used to be mighty faithful to his prayer-meeting, but old marster begun to be mighty mean to him. His wife lived on another plantation, and marster told Richard he had to give up that wife and take a woman on our place. Richard told old marster he did not want any other woman; he said he loved his wife and could never love any other woman. His wife was named Betty. I believe Richard would die for Betty. Sometimes Richard would slip off and go to see Betty, and marster told the patrollers every time they caught Richard on the plantation where Betty lived to beat him half to death. The patrollers had caught Richard many times, and had beat him mighty bad. So one night Richard heard the dogs coming in the woods near his wife's house, and he jumped out of his wife's window, and he went for dear life or death through the woods. He said he had to always pass over the bayou to go to his wife, but that night the patrollers were so hot behind him that he lost his way. He had a skiff he always went over in, but he forgot about the skiff when they were after him. Richard said he just took off every piece of clothes he had on and tied them around his neck and swam across the bayou. He lost his hat, and went without any all day in the field. Richard said when he got to the bayou he was wet with sweat, and it was one of the coldest nights he had ever felt in Louisiana. He said he had about two miles to go after he got over the bayou, and when he got across he just slipped on his clothes he had around his neck, and ran every step of the way to his own plantation. Sometimes they would catch Richard and drive four stakes in the ground, and they would tie his feet and hands to each one and beat him half to death. I tell you, sometimes he could not work. Marster did not care, for he had told Richard to take some of our women for a wife, but Richard would not do it. Richard loved Betty, and he would die for her."

"Did you say Richard was a Christian, Aunt Charlotte?"

"Yes; he used to pray and sing with us, many, many times, all the hymns Aunt Jane sung to us. I remember Richard used to sing:

> "'In the valley, in the valley,
>   There's a mighty cry to
> Jesus in the valley;
>   So weary, so tired, Lord, I wish
>   I was in heaven, hallelu.'"

Aunt Charlotte said: "Poor Richard! I reckon he is dead now. When the Yankees came he was one of the first ones to leave our place, and I never heard from him any more. I reckon if he is dead he is resting at last in heaven. O, he had so many trials in this cold, unfriendly world! But he never give up praying and trusting in the Lord. Sometimes when we all would be hoeing the cane we did not go home to dinner, but we had our victuals in a basket, and we ate under a shade-tree. When it was hot marster used to let us have one hour and a half at twelve o'clock. Then we used to have good times under the shade-trees. We used to talk of Aunt Jane Lee, and we would sing some of her hymns till we all would go to sleep."

CHAPTER V

GREAT TRIBULATIONS

The death of Lena—Her dying testimony—Aunt Charlotte's mistress
ties a servant by the thumbs—She returns and finds her dead.

"YOU remember I told you about Lena being one of our
sisters in our prayer-meetings," said Aunt Charlotte.

"Yes; I recollect, I believe, a great many names you have spoken to me about every time you came talking about your past unhappy life; and I must confess to you that I have enjoyed your conversation very much. I have concluded to write the story of your life in the cane-fields of Louisiana, and I desire to write it in your own words, as near as possible."

"La, me, child! I never thought any body would care enough for me to tell of my trials and sorrows in this world! None but Jesus knows what I have passed through."

"Tell me, Aunt Charlotte, about Lena."

"She died with small-pox, and we all grieved and missed her among us. I had to 'tend to Lena when she was sick. I was the only one that had the small-pox at that time. She told me when she first got sick she would not live. But she said, 'Charlotte, I have been working and praying for this hour. O,' she said, 'God has promised to lead all who will follow him. I have been toiling so long; now I'm about to cross over.' I said to Lena, 'Yes, my sister, Jesus stopped dying to redeem one soul on the cross. Remember how Aunt Jane used to read to us that Jesus promised the thief on the cross that he should be with him in paradise.' Lena asked me to sing, 'On Jordan's stormy banks I stand, and cast a wistful eye.' O, I can never forget Lena! She is in heaven this day, I believe. We learned that hymn from Aunt Jane Lee. Just before Lena died she said, 'Glory be to God and

16

the Lamb forever! Safe at last, safe at last!' These were her last words to me. I remember when old marster got mad with Lena he used to put her in jail all day on Sunday and give her nothing but bread and water to eat."

"Aunt Charlotte, my heart throbs with sympathy, and my eyes are filled with tears, whenever I hear you tell of the trials of yourself and others. I've read and heard very often of the hard punishments of the slaves in the South; but the half was never told."

"No, half of it aint been told. I could sit right here and tell you the trials and tribulations I have had to go through with my three marsters here in Louisiana, and it would be dark before I got half through with my own; but if I tried to tell of the sorrows of others, what I have seen here in Louisiana since I have been here, it would take me all the week, I reckon."

"But Aunt Charlotte, have you nothing good to tell? Did your master never show any sympathy for his slaves?"

"My dear child, if you believe me, I never got one dollar from my marster in my life. After rolling was over he would get big jugs of whisky and *make* us all drink at his house door, but after that nothing more but hard work and rough treatment from one year's end to the other.

"I want to tell you about poor Ella, old mistress's house servant. She was only twelve years old. Ella's mother did not live with her. Mistress had no more feeling for her than she had for a cat. She used to beat her and pull her ears till they were sore. She would crack her on the head with a key or any thing she could get her hands on till blood would ooze out of the poor child's head. Mistress's mother give Ella to her, and when Ella got to be about eighteen mistress got jealous of her and old marster. She used to punish Ella all sorts of ways. Sometimes she tied her up by her thumbs. She could do nothing to please mistress. She had been in the habit of tying Ella up, but one day she tied her up and left her, and when she went back she found Ella dead. She told old marster she did not intend to kill her, that she only wanted to punish her. Mistress and marster did not live good after she killed Ella, for a long time. Poor Ella! I don't know where she is to-day. She was a Catholic. You could always see her with her beads and cross in her pocket. She is in purgatory, I reckon; for the Catholics say the priest can hold mass and get any body out for so much money. But nobody held mass for Ella, and so she will have to stay in purgatory. But, I tell you, I believe there is only two places for us—heaven and torment. If we miss heaven we must be forever lost."

"Yes, Aunt Charlotte, that's the teaching of the Bible."

"Aunt Jane used to tell us, too, that the children of Israel was in Egypt in bondage, and that God delivered them out of Egypt; and she said he would deliver us. We all used to sing a hymn like this:

> "'My God delivered Daniel, Daniel, Daniel;
>   My God delivered Daniel,
>   And why not deliver me too?
>   He delivered Daniel from the lions' den,
>   Jonah from the belly of the whale,
>   The three Hebrew children from the fiery furnace,
>   And why not deliver me too?'

"O, you ought to hear Richard sing that hymn! I never can forget Aunt Jane, for when old marster used to be so hard on me it seemed I'd have to give up sometimes and die. But then the Spirit of God would come to me and fill my heart with joy. It seemed the more trials I had the more I could pray."

"Aunt Charlotte, you remind me of Pilgrim's Progress."

"Yes, I remember about Pilgrim traveling from the City of Destruction to the Celestial City."

I said, "His name was John Bunyan. He was confined in jail twelve years on account of his religion."

"Was he a slave too?"

"No; he was not a slave, but at the time he lived people were persecuted on account of their religious belief."

"Yes, my child, that's the way it is here in Louisiana. The most of the white people were Catholics around where I lived, and we poor darkies that did not believe in Catholic religion had to suffer on account of it. But that's the time a true child of God prays, when he gets in trouble. For I know the most peaceful hours were when marster would put me in jail all day Sunday. We used to sing this song:

>"'O, brother, where was you?
>O, brother, where was you?
>O, brother, where was you
>When the Lord come passing by?
>>Jesus been here,
>>O, he's been here;
>>He's been here
>>Soon in the morning;
>>Jesus been here,
>>And blest my soul and gone.'

"Yes, my dear child, that hymn filled me with joy many a time when I'd be in prison on Sunday. I'd sit all day singing and praying. I tell you, Jesus did come and bless me in there. I was sorry for marster. I wanted to tell him sometimes about how sweet Jesus was to my soul; but he did not care for nothing in this world but getting rich. He had a brother living in Georgia. I believe he did not believe in Catholic religion.

"We all knowed his brother from Georgia, because he used to always come out in rolling season to see us make sugar. He used to love to hear us sing. Once while he was out he took mighty sick, and I had to attend to him. He asked me to pray for him. I said, 'Yes, sir; I will pray for you, but you must touch the hem of the Saviour's garment yourself.' 'Yes,' he said, 'I am a Christian, and have been for many years.' We used to hear him sing, when he was riding over the field looking at the cane, one hymn he used to like. It was this:

>"'When my heart first believed,
>>What a joy I received,
>>What a heaven in Jesus's name!'

"I knowed that hymn, and it used to do me good to hear him sing Aunt Jane's hymns. He married a woman in Georgia; and he had lived there so long till he almost forgot how to speak French. Old marster did not like 'Merican people. Old mistress used to have balls on Sunday. She had me and her cook fixing all day Sunday for the ball on Sunday night sometimes. Mistress's religion did not make her happy like my religion did. I was a poor slave, and every body knowed I had religion, for it was Jesus with me every-where I went. I could never hear her talk about that heavenly journey."

CHAPTER VI

A KIND MISTRESS

Death of Aunt Charlotte's mistress—Second marriage of Aunt
Charlotte's master—George, one of Aunt Charlotte's fellow-
servants, beaten nearly to death and one eye put out for being
overheard talking about freedom.

"**M**Y mistress took sick with fever, and we all did not think
she was bad off. We knowed she had been used to being
sick now and then, but would soon be up. But she never left her
bed alive. They sent for the priest just before she died. He
greased her with something, I believe, and they say she took the
sacrament from the priest that day. But I am afraid she is lost.
She died just like she lived. Mistress did not live right, and she
did not die right. The old saying, 'Just as the tree falls, just so it
lies.' So many times I used to want to talk to her about her religion; but she seemed to know every thing, and I was a poor creature that knowed nothing but how to work for marster in the
cane-field. Marster had mass for mistress, I don't know how
many times; but what good did it do her soul?"

"None whatever, Aunt Charlotte; we must make our peace
with God before we leave the world. This world is our dressing-
room, and if we are not dressed up and prepared to meet God
when we die we can never enter the promised land; for there is
no preparation beyond the grave. The Bible tells us, 'Whatsoever
a man soweth, that shall he also reap.'"

"Yes," said Aunt Charlotte; "I have heard Aunt Jane say she used
to hear the preacher in Virginia preach that very text. She used to
say, 'The wages of sin is death; but the gift of God is eternal life.'"

"Why, Aunt Charlotte, she was equal to a preacher; she was
certainly above the average of colored women."

"Yes, my child, she was raised in Virginia, and she learned how to read before she came out here."

"Aunt Charlotte, at the death of your mistress did you all get on any better with your master?"

"No, my child; old marster always ruled that place. He went to Georgia and married a lady, and we all was mighty glad he married a 'Merican woman, because we thought we would be allowed to go to church. But, la, my child! she did not believe in Catholic religion, but old marster ruled her and she could not do what she wanted. It would do your soul good to hear her sing the hymns when she came to our place. Sometimes on Sunday mornings she would go out in the flower-garden, and we would hear her singing,

> "'Happy day, happy day,
> When Jesus washed my sins away.'

"They did not live good together. I always believed he was sorry he married her, for she was not Catholic. I used to see her crying when he would leave her and go off. He was rich, but that did not make his last wife happy. She was a pretty young woman, but she soon began to look old after she came to our place. She would let us have our little meetings, but he would not allow her to have any thing to do with us. I liked old marster's last wife. She used to come in the kitchen on Sundays and talk about religion. She wanted to go to 'Merican church, but it was so far away she could not go often. It was about twenty miles away from our place. Sometimes, though, she went. I remember she told me that the minister took for his text one Sunday morning, 'Rest for the people of God.' I said to mistress, 'La! how I wish I could heard that preached!' She said to me, 'Yes, Charlotte, it would do your soul good to hear that minister preach.' I knowed mistress could not let me go to church. Marster didn't like 'Merican or Protestant religion, and he didn't want none of us to go. I just tell you, my child, Catholic religion and 'Merican religion can't go together. A woman does mighty bad business marrying a Catholic man if she believes in 'Merican religion. They don't live peaceful together. We never had any more dancing on

Sunday nor Monday after marster married that 'Merican woman. Sometimes marster's kinfolks would come to see his last wife on Sunday evening, but they did not have any pleasure together. You know oil and water wont mix, and just so with the Catholic and 'Merican religions. They believe our religion is nothing."

"If the Catholics could feel that spark of heavenly love that pervades the soul of every true converted child of God, Aunt Charlotte, they would never doubt the American religion."

"I believe so, my child. When the Yankees came I left the plantation, and I don't know what become of mistress after I left her; but I think of her now, and would be so glad to see her. If she is dead I believe she is at rest, for she used to talk about that Christian journey so much."

"Yes, Aunt Charlotte, I knew of white women who were truly converted here in the South, and who took pleasure in teaching the colored people the Scriptures. I knew, in the State of Georgia, white families who would compel their slaves to attend church on Sundays and would not allow them to work on that day. If they did not attend church they would go out in the colored people's cabins and read the Bible to them very often on Sundays and explain it to them. I don't mean to say that the whites did this as a general thing, but many of them did."

"But how could they have good religion and keep us poor darkies in bondage and beat us half to death?"

"Well, Aunt Charlotte, I am hardly able to answer you satisfactorily, I must confess, for when I pause and think over the hard punishments of the slaves by the whites, many of whom professed to be Christians, I am filled with amazement. Religion fills our souls with love for God and humanity. The Bible, moreover, says, 'We know we have passed from death unto life, because we love the brethren.' And you know as a rule there were comparatively few colored people during the period of slavery, or even now, but what are members of some Christian denomination. So they were their brethren through Christ.

"Aunt Charlotte, did you slaves know what brought on this last war?"

"Yes, child; we heard people say the Yankees was fighting to free us. But, my child, it was death for us poor darkies to talk about freedom. We had a man on our place named George. Marster did not like him much, no how, and one day he over-heard George talking about freedom; and, I tell you, he half killed him that day. He beat George a while, and then would make the driver beat him a while. They say they give George nine hundred lashes and then made him wash all over in salt water. While he was whipping him he put out one of George's eyes. Poor George didn't have but one eye after that. But, let me tell you, it was not three months after that before marster bought a fine horse, and he used to drive him to his buggy all the time. Old marster loved that horse better than he loved his wife, I think. One morning he was driving out, and the horse got scared at something and run away, broke the buggy all to pieces, throwed marster flat on the ground and broke his leg. Old marster never did walk without a crutch after that. I tell you I was sorry for marster, for he suffered so much when he was down in the bed from his broken leg. But I thought no good would ever come of him when he put out George's eye."

"Yes," said I, "we read in the Bible that 'fools, because of their transgression, and because of their iniquities, are afflicted.'"

CHAPTER VII

BROKEN-DOWN FREEDMEN

Aunt Charlotte splitting rails—In Sunday-school—Joe Sims, a run-away, sleeping in the woods with rattlesnakes—Eating out of trash-boxes.

"Aunt Charlotte, people who never knew any thing about slave-life in the South can hardly credit the reports that have been circulated by those who have resided here. For it seems to me that the terrible treatment the slaves received from the hands of their masters was more than any human being could bear."

"But, my child, every word is true. I can't tell you half what my two eyes have seen since I have been in Louisiana. The white folks did not take the niggers for nothing more than brutes. They would take more time with fine horses, and put them up to rest. We poor darkies were never allowed to rest. I have split rails many and many a day, and sometimes my back would almost break when I'd have to roll logs, but I had to keep pulling along. When night came I could hardly drag one foot before the other. I'd go to my bed, and it would be wet where it leaked through the top of the house, and I'd just fall in it and would not know it was wet with water till next morning. I'd find leeches sticking to my legs, and blood would be all on my feet. I'd get them in the woods cutting wood. I tell you, if you get a leech on you it will draw like a blister. When I came to my house at night I was too tired to eat. I went to bed a many time hungry—was too broke down to cook my supper after working all the day hard."

"Why, I can't see what kept you alive, Aunt Charlotte, till now!"

"The dear Lord and Saviour kept me alive, and he is still taking care of me. Ever since I came to town I never miss going to church; and the other Sunday morning I went into the Sunday-school before church began, and I heard the children sing something like this:

> "'All the way my Saviour leads me.'

And when them children sang that it filled my eyes with tears, for I just thought how good the Lord had been to me. He had brought me through so much hardship, and I said, 'Here I am, Lord, blest to sit down and hear singing and preaching.' It was the first time I had ever heard that hymn, and I thought it was so sweet to my soul."

"Yes," I said, "it's one of my favorite hymns."

"Wont you get your book and read it for me if you please?"

"Here it is:

> " 'All the way my Saviour leads me;
>   What have I to ask beside?
> Can I doubt his tender mercy,
>   Who through life has been my guide?
> Heavenly peace, divinest comfort,
>   Here by faith in him I dwell!
> For I know whate'er befall me,
>   Jesus doeth all things well.
>
> " 'All the way my Saviour leads me;
>   Cheers each winding path I tread;
> Gives me grace for every trial;
>   Feeds me with the living bread;
> Though my weary steps may falter,
>   And my soul athirst may be,
> Gushing from the Rock before me,
>   Lo! a spring of joy I see.
>
> " 'All the way my Saviour leads me;
>   O, the fullness of his love!
> Perfect rest to me is promised
>   In my Father's house above;

> When my spirit, clothed immortal,
> Wings its flight to realms of day,
> This my song through endless ages—
> Jesus led me all the way.'"

"O, bless the Lord for the chance of hearing those words! They suit my case. I want to sing that very hymn in glory. Yes, 'Jesus led me all the way.' Sometimes I don't know where I'll get a piece of bread when I get up in the morning, but still I'm living and praising God. We poor old colored people were turned off the plantations without any thing in this world to go on—turned out like sheep in the woods. Mrs. B—— promised me last week if I'd come around and wash dishes for her every day she would give me the scraps she had left always at meals. I thank the Lord for that much. I don't need much in this world, no how—just enough to keep soul and body together. I know I can't stay here much longer, I don't want nothing in this world. If I can just get a little coffee every morning and a piece of bread I am satisfied."

"Aunt Charlotte, you can't always get a little coffee and bread?"

"No, child."

"Why, it seems you could get enough to do among the different families here in this town."

"No, bless your soul; the most of the white people don't want me—they say I am too old. I can't see how to work, and what I could do they wont let me."

"Aunt Charlotte, I see a great many old, feeble-looking men and women around in this place."

"Yes, many of them just like me—nobody to help them, and they are too old to do work, and just go wandering about picking up any thing they can get. Poor old Brother Joe Sims picks up, one half of his time, scraps out of the trash-boxes. He picks up rags for a living, and I have seen him eating out of the box of trash sometimes. Brother Joe is a member of our church; he never misses to come to church on Sundays. He came from Virginia too. He used to tell me how he stayed in the woods after he was sold out here. He said once his marster got after him to whip him and he would not let him do it. He said he run away in the woods for a long time. Brother Joe said he had a bed made of moss and limbs of trees in the woods. He said every day he would go off and get something to eat wherever he could, and then go back to his moss bed at night. You ought to hear him tell about the rattlesnakes that used to keep him company in the woods. He said the snakes got so used to him that they stayed under his moss bed at night. Sometimes he could hear them turning over under him. The snakes would go off in the day and come back at night. He could kill them if he wanted to, but he was glad to have them for company.

"You see, my child, God will take care of his people," said Aunt Charlotte. "He will hear us when we cry. True, we can't get any thing to eat sometimes, but trials make us pray more. I just tell you, I don't sleep all night no night. I can't; for the Spirit of God wakes me up between midnight and day, and I just gets right down on my knees and tells my Father all about my trials here below. We all are free, but we can't stop praying; we must keep on; we aint out of Egypt yet. We have been let loose, and now we are just marching on to a better land."

"Aunt Charlotte, it really makes me feel happy to hear you express your faith in the goodness of God. He has wrought wonderful works for the colored people here. He has raised up friends all through the North for them. Never was education so cheap as now. School-houses are being built all through the South for them. The money is being given by philanthropic Christians to educate the colored children. Education and morality will lift the colored people up out of the degradation in which they have been kept so long by their educated white Christian brethren."

"But, my child, so few of the children can go to school about here. We have school six months in this town, and you can see the children coming for a little while, and then they have to leave to go to work in the cane-field. All are poor, and they have to work to get something to eat. The children learn to read a little, and after that they leave school. I know a few go off to New Orleans sometimes to school, but only two or three. O, I wish the good times had come when I was young!"

CHAPTER VIII

THE CURSE OF WHISKY

The Methodist Episcopal Church—The colored people and whisky-drinking—When the Yankees came to Louisiana—The end of Aunt Charlotte's story.

"AUNT Charlotte, which church are you a member of here?"
"I am a member of the Methodist Church. Our minister said the other Sunday the Methodist Church divided on account of slavery many years ago, and that the old mother-Church never failed to crush out slavery at every turn. It seems to me every Christian that honors God in the pardoning of their sins ought to agree to every thing that is holy and good. How could any Christian man believe it was right to sell and buy us poor colored people just like we was sheep? I tell you, I have seen black people, in slave-time, drove along—may be one hundred in a drove—just like hogs to be sold. Sometimes men were sold from their wives and mothers from their children. I saw a white man in Virginia sell his own child he had by a colored woman there. They say a 'Merican man never would take care of his children he would have in slave-time by the black women, as a Frenchman would here in Louisiana. Old marster used to say niggers did not have a soul, and I reckon all the white folks thought so too."

"Aunt Charlotte, education and religion taught them better."

"Yes, child; for when I first got religion I did not want to hurt an ant. Every thing was love, joy, and peace with me. I sometimes think my people don't pray like they used to in slavery. You know when any child of God gets trouble that's the time to try their faith. Since freedom it seems my people don't trust in the

Lord as they used to. 'Sin is growing bold, and religion is grow-ing cold.' That's what our minister says sometimes."

"Aunt Charlotte, I am told that the colored people are suffer-ing more from the habit of indulging in strong drink than any thing else here in the South."

"Yes, my dear child; in the time of slavery one hardly knew what whisky was in some places; but since freedom we see men and women drunk. About a year ago I went out to a plantation near this town and I saw two hundred liquor-barrels emptied and laying around on the place. All the planters keep whisky for the laborers, and they spend more money for drink than they do for any thing else. They don't get much for their work, no way, and I can't see how the hired men can drink so much whisky."

"Aunt Charlotte, how much are the men paid per day?"

"They get only fifty and sixty cents a day. Some of the men have a wife and four or five children to take care of. They have their wife to help them, but, la, me! the wife's help is next to nothing in the field. The women can't get as much as the men, no way, although they go out and work hard all day long and keep up with the men too."

"I can't see, Aunt Charlotte, how any man who has four or five children can afford to drink when he makes only fifty and sixty cents per day!"

"Well, I tell you how they do. They always have an account open in the plantation store, and they allow them to get any thing they want from the store. If they come out in debt at the end of the year they work on the next year and pay it. Sometimes they find at the end of the year they owe the planter fifty dollars for whisky. Why, my dear child, I know children on some of them plantations ten years old never had a pair of shoes to keep their feet off the cold, frosty ground since they were born."

"Yes, I am induced to believe, Aunt Charlotte, that whisky is causing more suffering among the colored people than slavery, or as much, any way. The temperance society that has been lately organized in this town is destined to do much good among the colored people."

"Yes; the preacher holds temperance meeting every Sunday

evening now in our church after preaching. It would do your heart good to hear our sisters make little temperance speeches after preaching on Sunday evenings. We had a sister named Ellen, and her husband was named Jack. Sister Ellen couldn't read, but she would make her speech whenever her time came around on Sunday evening. She said, 'Brothers and sisters, I don't know much and can't say much, but let me tell you all, since Jack got in this little society the preacher started here he is changed all over. Why, Jack used to sleep in the gutters of water one half of his time at night. I used to have to pick Jack up almost every night and carry him home. He's got religion too. Jack is a good man. He did not care any thing for his children, and I could not get a cup of coffee one half of my time when he drank gin; but now I get coffee, sugar, and shoes, and he takes care of his children too. Now,' she said, 'come up, all you men sitting over yonder, come and join this little society.' We all would laugh at Sister Ellen, for she seemed so earnest in her talk. She would shake her fist and knock on the railing around the altar whenever she got up to speak. She did not mind us laughing, though; she went right on. One time after she got through speaking about ten men and women came up and joined the 'little society.'"

"Aunt Charlotte, it is a great pity, and, indeed, a great sin, for the planters to keep whisky on their plantations for their laborers. It's a temptation set before them."

"Yes; I always thought so too; but the planters don't care just so they get them to do the work good. They don't get too drunk to work through the week; but on Sundays they lay about almost dead drunk on some plantations. I tell you, I am afraid whisky will ruin my people yet."

"I trust not, Aunt Charlotte. There is a great temperance movement going on throughout this country, and we are destined to see good results from it. We hope to have a law to prevent the sale of any intoxicating drinks. It may be many years, but I believe we shall have it."

"I trust in the Lord to bring it to pass. Our people suffer more than any body, for we were turned loose without any thing, and we got no time to waste. We must get education, and, above all things in this world, get religion, and then we will be ladies and gentlemen."

"Yes; I believe religion and education will lift them upon a level with any other of the civilized races on earth. It's true we see so much prejudice manifested almost every-where we go; but we must wait on the Lord. He has promised to carry us through."

Aunt Charlotte said: "It makes me so glad to see my people going to school. Never did I think to see these good times! White people would not let us learn the book in slave-time. I used to want to learn when I was young, but they would not even let us have a book to study in. La, child! when the Yankees came out here our eyes began to open, and we have been climbing ever since. Whenever I see a Yankee it makes me mighty glad, for I just feel that God sent them down here to set us free. When the war was going on I heard they was fighting for us. I tell you, when it was going on I did not cease to pray. We done the praying and the Yankees done the fighting, and God heard our prayers 'way down here in these cane-fields. Many times I have bowed down between the cane-rows, when the cane was high, so nobody could see me, and would pray in the time of the war! I used to say, 'O, my blessed Lord, be pleased to hear my cry; set me free, O my Lord, and I will serve you the balance of my days.' I knowed God had promised to hear his children when they cry, and he heard us way down here in Egypt."

Thus ends the story of Aunt Charlotte's life in the cane-fields of Louisiana. But the half cannot be told.

CHAPTER IX

JOHN AND LORENDO

Work to be done—John Goodwin and Lorendo, his wife—Uncle
  John's little brother washed away by the rain.

IF missionary preachers and teachers are needed in the heart
  of Africa they are needed in this Southland too, among these
millions of lately emancipated souls. It is true we find in the
cities and towns that the colored people have schools of some
sort; but, leave the railroads twenty or thirty miles, and we
behold the heathen at our doors. They are reared up in super-
stition, the same as before the war, in a great many places. They
need well-educated ministers, for the blind cannot lead the
blind. I am glad, however, to note that the Methodists, the
Baptists, the Congregationalists, and the other denominations
are doing very much toward the education of colored men for
the Christian ministry. May God, who guided Israel, continue to
direct the hearts of the philanthropic Christians every-where to
turn a listening ear to the sad cry of these needy souls whom
Christ died to save.

> "Whatsoever thing thou doest
> To the least of mine and lowest,
> That thou doest unto me."

It is, indeed, a mystery to those who have witnessed the cruelty
of the whites in the South toward the poor, ignorant, innocent,
degraded, and helpless people whom God, in his own good time,
has liberated. Here, with an open Bible, a Christian land of pros-
perity for the Caucasian; but, alas! what for the negro? O, bishops
and ministers of every Christian denomination in this Southland,

how can you, as heralds of Jesus, sit quietly by and see the needs of seven millions or more of human souls crying in the valley of sin and sorrow and not give a listening ear to them? Go out into the highways and hedges and tell them of Jesus, mighty to save. Do you preach that Jesus tasted death for *every man?* How strange that here in the South the Methodist Church and the Baptist Church seem ready and willing to send missionaries to other countries, and are not willing to extend a helping hand to these needy souls who have served them so long and faithfully! Behold your "brethren in black" at your doors; arise and let them in. And the least you do for Jesus will be precious in his sight.

During my stay in the town of ——, where I met Charlotte Brooks, I met another slave who had formerly lived in the State of Georgia. He was a cooper by trade, and had a wife and three children. John Goodwin was his name. Here in the South it is considered by the black people a mark of respect to address the older men and women as "uncle" and "aunt"; and, as Mr. Goodwin was aged and gray, I, too, soon learned to address him as "Uncle John." So one day, as he passed by, I called to him and said:

"Uncle John, Aunt Charlotte tells me that you formerly lived in the State of Georgia. I came from there when I was young, and am therefore very glad to meet you. Wont you come around to see me some time and have a good talk about our native home?"

He said: "Yes, ma'am; I'd be mighty glad to come 'round and have a good long talk about my old home. It makes me glad to see any body from Georgia. I came out here to Louisiana long before the war begun. When my old marster died all his property was divided among his children, and my marster's oldest daughter drawed me, and she married and moved here to Louisiana."

Uncle John then bowed his head and said, "Good-morning, ma'am."

He promised that he would come in a few days and bring his wife, Lorendo, with him. Sure enough, in a few days in comes Uncle John and his wife. As he entered he said:

"Here's my wife, Mrs. A. She is a Creole woman; her name is Lorendo. I left my other wife in Georgia when the white folks brought me out here."

What a great pity that husbands and wives should thus have been separated!

"That's the cry all over the South, Uncle John," I said.

"Yes, ma'am; I thought when I left wife and children in Georgia it would break my heart; but, bless the Lord, I'm still on pleading terms of mercy."

I said, "Did you find by moving to this State you fared any better?"

"No , ma'am; the white folks were bad every-where. The only difference I found out here is the white people did not regard the Sabbath day. Why, ma'am, they would make the darkies work all day Sunday sometimes when they was pushed up with the grass in the cane."

"Yes, I've learned they desecrated the Sabbath to a fearful extent; and even now, Uncle John, we see almost every body selling and buying on Sunday. I presume it is a habit that they have indulged so long that they hardly know how to discontinue it. Even among the Protestant churches we find many who disregard the Sabbath in this State."

Aunt Lorendo said: "Why, ma'am, I never knowed nothing else but buying and selling all my life on Sunday. I was born right here in Louisiana, and the priest and every body else always got whatever they wanted on Sunday. I did not know it was wrong."

I asked Uncle John if he knew Aunt Charlotte Brooks.

He said: "Yes, ma'am; I been knowing Sister Charlotte for a long time. She is a good member of our church here. She suffers with rheumatism mighty bad."

"Yes, Uncle John; I've learned to love her since my stay here. She has spent many hours with me telling of her slave-life in this State. I don't think there are many women who have gone through the hardship that she has and endured it. She must have had an extraordinary constitution."

"Why, ma'am, Sister Charlotte just suffered like the most of us did. Sometimes you could find white people who treated we poor slaves right good; but it was not often. Why, in my young days I used to pick cotton all day and half of the night. My marster used to set a tree on fire for us to see how to pick cotton. I have picked as much as three and four hundred pounds of cotton in one day a many a time. I tell you, my old marster used to work us half to death trying to get rich."

In many portions of the State of Georgia there are high and rugged hills. Here we find low and marshy land, and it is therefore very unhealthy for weak and feeble persons, especially those who suffer with any throat or lung troubles. Uncle John related many thrilling accounts of his slave-life in the State of Georgia. He had a baby brother named Jim, and his mother, having to work in the field every day, was compelled to leave her children. It was a very common habit, in some portions of the State, to build the cabins upon the high hills with earth floors; and Uncle John's mother always left the baby in the cradle, during the day, all alone. So one day she was in the field plowing, and a heavy rain-storm came up, and she hastened to her cabin as soon as she could; for she knew her dear little babe was there, only two years of age, and no one with it, and it poured down through the cabin, and also washed through it, like a branch of water.

Uncle John said: "I tell you, when my mammy got to her cabin she saw where little Jim had been in the cradle; but he was out and gone, she did not know where. Mammy saw where the rain had washed clear through her house, and she said she knowed the branch was not far from the house, and big gutters all the way between her house and the creek; so she went down toward the creek as fast as she could, and there she found little Jim being rolled over and over by the rain. Mammy said Jim was almost to the creek when she took him up. My mammy cried a while and she prayed a while when she found her child that day."

Uncle John declared that the little baby boy who was picked up almost one fourth of a mile from her cabin that stormy day is now living in the State of Alabama. He is a local preacher there.

"My mammy had to work hard all day long with all the balance of the men. She was a mighty smart woman," said Uncle John. "After working all day in the cotton-field she would come home and work half of the night for herself and children. She used to wash, patch, spin, and cook for the next day to carry out in the field."

CHAPTER X

A CONVERTED CATHOLIC

Going to church on Sunday in Georgia—Ill-treatment of Uncle John's
daughter—Aunt Lorendo's second visit—Her conversion from
Romanism—Her Cousin Albert to be hung—Hattie runs away to
the woods and gives birth to a child there.

I ASKED Uncle John if he did not find it hard, after moving to
Louisiana, that he could not attend church as he used to in
Georgia.

"Yes, madam; I missed the good preaching I used to hear in
Georgia. We all walked a many a time ten and twelve miles to go
to church there on Sunday. My mammy used to cook on
Saturday for us all to carry with us on Sunday; and we all would
get up before day on Sunday morning and start off to church. I
tell you, we would walk a while and rest a while under the shade
of the trees on the road-side. Sometimes we would get to the
church before ten o'clock. They always begun preaching at
eleven o'clock, and we'd be afraid we would not get there in
time. My wife in Georgia was named Nancy; she got religion
while the minister was preaching. I had religion before my wife
did. Nancy had been praying for a long time. She used to go
away off in the woods to pray. I went in the woods many times
to pray; I thought I could pray better in the swamp."

Uncle John said: "I remember until this day the text that minister took that Sunday when Nancy got religion. It was, 'Behold,
I stand at the door and knock.' I tell you, ma'am, Nancy shouted,
and was so happy we could hardly get her home that evening.
She shouted all along the road as we walked. We all got happy
on our way back that night, and I do believe it was ten o'clock

before we reached home. Nancy cried out in church when she was converted, and said, 'Glory be to God and the Lamb forever! I am washed clean by the blood of Jesus.'"

Uncle John said: "Poor Nancy! I reckon she is dead now. She was our white folks' cook. We had a little girl ten years old; she waited in the house. They would blindfold her and beat my poor child half to death. I tell you, my heart would bleed sometimes when I'd see how my child was treated. I could do nothing for my wife and children. I was not allowed to open my mouth."

Uncle John could hardly suppress the tears from his eyes while relating the sad condition of his wife and the inhuman abuse of his daughter when he left them in Georgia, although it had been many years. He said, "O, if I could only see my children once more!"

He left me that evening with the promise that he would come to see me again, and that he would have his wife visit me too. Aunt Lorendo said, "I know where you live now, and will stop to see you sometimes when I pass." I told her I thanked her, and that I should be pleased to have her stop at any time. I said, "It affords me real pleasure to have yourself and husband relate your trials and sorrows that you both had to endure so long."

It was not long before Aunt Lorendo called again. As she entered the door I said: "Good morning, Aunt Lorendo; how are you feeling?"

"I am pretty well," she said.

I asked, "How is Uncle John?"

"O, he is well as might be expected for an old man. You know he passed through so much hardship in slavery, he will never feel well till he gets home. He caught so much cold and is so painful he can't hardly rest at night. But," she added, "I trust we both will rest by and by."

"Yes, Aunt Lorendo, the Bible promises that there is 'rest for the people of God.' And it affords us joy to know that although we have trials and tribulations here we who prove faithful till death shall enter that 'rest prepared for the people of God.'"

"Yes, ma'am; I used to be Catholic, but I never knowed how good the 'Merican religion was till I married John. He was a member of the 'Merican church, and he got me to go with him on Sundays to his church; and the more I went the more I liked it. I made my first communion when I was fifteen years old in the Catholic Church, and I was a Catholic for a long time. I tell you, I used to think no other religion was good like mine. I made fun of the 'Merican religion; but now, ever since I been changed, I feel like I been new born. I tell you that 'Merican religion makes any body feel happy all over; it runs all through you, down from your head to the very soles of your feet! But Catholic religion is all doings and no feeling in the heart."

"Aunt Lorendo, when you were a Catholic did you always confess every thing to the priest?"

"Yes, ma'am; I'd tell the priest every thing I did wicked. But, I tell you, one time I had a cousin that told the priest he wanted to get free, and asked him to pray to God to set him free, and, bless your soul, ma'am, the priest was about to have my cousin hung. The priest told my cousin's marster about it, and they was talking strong about hanging my cousin. They had my cousin up and made him tell who had told him any thing about freedom. But the priest managed some way to save my poor cousin. Madam, I tell you, from that day on I could not follow my Catholic religion like I had. You know the Catholics always tell the priest every thing; they talk to him like a father; and so it was with my cousin. He would tell the priest every thing. He never thought he would tell on him."

"Why, Aunt Lorendo, don't you know the Catholics were bitterly opposed to the emancipation of the slaves? Why, the pope was the only power in the world that recognized the Confederacy. They assisted powerfully in carrying on the civil war. It is strange, however, that we find that here in the South among the Catholic churches we don't see the caste prejudice so clearly manifested among all the other denominations; nevertheless, they believe God has made the black man to serve the white man.

"Aunt Lorendo, Aunt Charlotte has spent many hours with me telling of her slave-life here in Louisiana, and as you were born and reared here perhaps the revelation of your experiences will be as thrilling as hers. I must say that she has caused tears to flow from my eyes many a day while relating her hardships."

"Yes," replied Aunt Lorendo; "we come through so much hardship sometimes I wonder why we poor darkies did not all die out in slave-time. They used to run away in the woods and stay till all the clothes was off their backs. Why, ma'am, I know one time, right in my neighborhood, one woman—her mistress always had the overseer beating her—her name was Hattie—she used to run away and live in the woods for three and four weeks at a time. I remember I was out in the field hoeing cane in slave-time, and as I was getting toward the end of my row of cane I heard somebody over the fence in the woods calling me, and at first I did not know what to do; but as I looked up through the fence I saw it was Hattie. Madam, if you believe me, Hattie was almost naked that day! She asked me to give her something to eat; and I did give her all I had in my bucket. Hattie said, 'Lorendo, I had my child here in the woods; it is dead and I buried it in a piece of my frockshirt.' I said, 'La! Hattie, how in the world did you do by yourself?' She said, 'I don't know, Lorendo. All I can tell, God took care of me in these woods. O,' she said, 'I have so many trials with my mistress. I try to satisfy her, but nothing I do pleases her. I left my home, I reckon, two months. I tore all my clothes off of me. See! I am almost naked.' I said, 'Hattie, why did you run away?' 'Because, Lorendo,' she said, 'old mistress came up to me one morning and went to beating me with a big iron key all over my head, and I tell you, she almost give me a fit. I give her one hard slap and left her. I knowed marster would almost kill me, and I left for the woods before he came home.'"

I asked Aunt Lorendo if Hattie had a husband; she said no, that Hattie had two children by her master's son, and she reckoned the one Hattie had given birth to in the woods was by his son too. Hattie wanted to get married to one of the men on the place, but the master would not let her, because he wanted her for his son.

"Well, Aunt Lorendo, what finally became of Hattie?"

"O, bless you, the patrollers at last caught her with the nigger-hounds one day when we was all coming out in the field, and we met poor Hattie. They had caught her that morning. Madam, I remember just like it was yesterday. There was six white men and ten hounds. All the white men was on horses, and poor Hattie was in front barefooted, the dogs behind her. Hattie was almost naked that morning; blood was all on her feet as she was walking along. I saw all of it with my own two eyes. O, how sorry I felt for poor Hattie! I heard when they got her home her marster put her in stocks every night and would beat her every morning. Hattie at last died from punishment, I believe."

Now, my readers, these are not imaginary thoughts, but they were actually related to me. While I pen these lines I can hardly suppress the tears when I picture to my mind a poor woman marching before six men, six horses, and ten blood-hounds with blood oozing from her feet. There were none to care for her or give a friendly word in her behalf. Poor creature, she had given birth to a child in the woods, being compelled to wander about like a wild beast in the forest on account of the inhuman treatment of the white man in this Bible land of ours! Just you imagine the poor creature, a precious soul in the sight of God, no doubt, this temple of the living God, being driven by blood-hounds, bruised and mangled as she marched before them. And with all that she was carried home and put in stocks at night and beaten *every* morning. On being asked how she got on in the woods without any human help she said, "I don't know; all I can tell you, God took care of me."

Dear Christian reader, can we doubt the presence of God with her? Did he not say, "Lo, I am with you always, even unto the end?" He has promised to guide us safely home if we will only follow him. Surely "He is a Rock in a weary land!" Glory be to God for all of his precious promises. Hattie could have cried out:

> "But with thee is mercy found,
> Balm to heal my every wound;
> Soothe, O soothe this troubled breast,
> Give the weary wanderer rest."

Aunt Lorendo's visits proved a source of much pleasure, as did Aunt Charlotte's many welcome visits.

CHAPTER XI

PRISON HORRORS

Uncle John taking lessons—Andersonville horrors—Blood-hounds—
Silas bitten by blood-hounds and eaten by buzzards.

UNCLE John always made it a habit to stop in on Saturday evenings. He was a steward of his church, and as he could not read very well he said he had made up his mind to study and try to learn more. He wanted to learn to read the Bible and hymn-book, anyhow, he said. He had to lead prayer-meeting in his church very often, and he said it would do him so much good if he could only read his Bible and hymn-book; so he employed me to teach him. I must confess Uncle John was pretty hard to teach. His mind was blunted, no doubt, and, having to work hard every day, and old and feeble as he was, I did not expect much of him. He decided that the first thing I must do was to read a chapter in the Bible, and also to read a hymn, saying he wanted to get them "by heart." His favorite hymns were: "Show pity, Lord," "How firm a foundation," "Must I be to judgment brought?" and "Try us, O God."

He would say: "La, Mrs. A., if I only had these good times in my young days! But I tell you, ma'am, I am glad I'm blest to see freedom! How many of my poor people died in slave-time and never knowed nothing but hard work all their life-time! I know," he said, "my poor Nancy is dead, and buried somewhere in Georgia. She worked hard all of her life-time, for the white folks never knowed what rest was. Sometimes I dream of all of my people I left in Georgia. It seems I can see my mammy in my sleep, and she comes right up beside my bed and talks with me sometimes. I know she is in heaven, for she used to be always talking about heaven when I was with her."

I said: "It would afford you so much joy to see your children once more; I reckon they are still living."

He said: "Yes, ma'am; I reckon if they is still living they is all married; but the white folks was so bad in slave-time I expect they all is dead. They used to run black people down with nigger-hounds, and would let the dogs bite them all over."

"Yes, Uncle John; your wife spent several hours not long ago telling of a poor woman that lived there near her plantation who was caught by the dogs, and she said the last she saw of the woman she was bleeding from dog-bites."

"Yes, ma'am; the white folks was bad here in Louisiana, but I think they was worse in Georgia for blood-hounds."

"Why, Uncle John," I said, "it looks as if allowing the dogs to bite them would bring on hydrophobia, and thereby cause a great many deaths among the slaves?"

"Yes; they did die often; but I always thought they died from being worked to death. Why, ma'am, I have seen poor colored men bleeding and dying from dog-bites. Once right in Georgia I saw a man where he crawled 'way off from his plantation and died under a shade-tree. Madam, that poor man had iron around his feet when we found him, and the buzzards had almost eaten his body up. I knowed the poor man; his name was Silas. He had run away and was caught by the dogs one morning, and his marster came up to him while he was fighting with the dogs, and Silas give one dog a blow and almost killed him. The hound was one of the best ones his marster had. Madam, Silas's marster got off of his horse right there where they caught him and beat Silas with his pistol all over for nothing because he would not let the dog bite him. He made the dogs bite Silas all over his body. The dogs bit him under the throat. When he got Silas home he put him in irons, but Silas could not walk. Silas was almost dead when his marster put the irons on him."

Uncle John said: "Poor Silas! I will never forget how I went out one Sunday morning and found him laying dead under that big oak-tree. He had a wife and six or seven children. He lived on one of the plantations in Georgia. We used to go to church on Sundays together. O, how he used to love that hymn, 'How firm a foundation!' He knowed every word of it by heart," said Uncle John. "We used to hear the white people sing it at church."

I asked Uncle John if Silas's master allowed him to attend church, and he said:

"Why, yes, ma'am; he used to let his slaves go to church on Sunday, and he went too; but that did not keep our white people from beating us through the week. They took sacrament in the morning, and we colored people took it in the evening."

"You were never allowed to take the sacrament with your masters?"

"No, ma'am; we been always separated here, and I reckon when we get up yonder in glory they will want to be separated," said Uncle John.

"No; there is no separation in glory. We read in the third chapter of Galatians, twenty-sixth to twenty-eighth verses: 'For ye are all the children of God by faith in Christ Jesus. For as many of you as have been baptized into Christ have put on Christ. There is neither Jew nor Greek, there is neither bond nor free, there is neither male nor female: for ye are all one in Christ Jesus.' Thus you see and hear what the Bible says: 'We are all one.'

> "'God is faithful; he will never
> Break his covenant sealed in blood;
> Signed when our Redeemer died;
> Sealed when he was glorified.' "

"Well," said Uncle John, "how in the world could the whites know the word of God, and so many used to seem to have religion, and yet treat us poor people just like the brutes?"

"I fear that a very few slave-holders had religion, Uncle John. If they had any at all it was not the Bible religion. Nevertheless, I do say there were some good white people who did not brutalize their slaves. But I regret to say that there were very few. They would punish them in many ways. If they did not kill them outright they killed them by brutalizing them. And we know that no murderers can enter that 'rest' prepared for the people of God unless they repent."

"They used to go to church," said Uncle John, "in Georgia, and I have seen them happy, too; but, madam, they would come right back from church and beat us all the week and make us work ourselves nearly to death."

"Uncle John, that was inconsistent with the teaching of the Bible. The Spirit of God is love, peace, joy, and contentment."

"Madam, I have talked so long this evening I will not say my lessons; but will you please read that hymn I love so much?"

" 'How firm a foundation,' Uncle John?"

"Yes, ma'am."

"Here it is:

> " 'How firm a foundation, ye saints of the Lord,
> Is laid for your faith in his excellent word!
> What more can he say, than to you he hath said,
> To you, who for refuge to Jesus have fled?
>
> " 'Fear not, I am with thee, O be not dismayed,
> For I am thy God, I will still give thee aid;
> I'll strengthen thee, help thee, and cause thee to stand,
> Upheld by my gracious, omnipotent hand.
>
> " 'When through the deep waters I call thee to go,
> The rivers of sorrow shall not overflow;
> For I will be with thee thy trials to bless,
> And sanctify to thee thy deepest distress.
>
> " 'When through fiery trials thy pathway shall lie,
> My grace, all-sufficient, shall be thy supply,
> The flames shall not hurt thee; I only design
> Thy dross to consume, and thy gold to refine.
>
> " 'E'en down to old age all my people shall prove
> My sovereign, eternal, unchangeable love;
> And when hoary hairs shall their temples adorn,
> Like lambs they shall still in my bosom be borne.
>
> " 'The soul that on Jesus hath leaned for repose,
> I will not, I will not desert to his foes;
> That soul, though all hell shall endeavor to shake,
> I'll never, no never, no never forsake!' "

Uncle John said: "O, bless the Lord! how often I heard that hymn sung in Georgia! Silas, poor man, did love it too. Madam, I do believe the angels came for Silas that day he crawled out under that big oak-tree and died there. You remember I told you we lived 'joining plantations, and many times I used to see him on his knees praying and praising God at twelve o'clock in the cotton-field. O, yes; I expect to meet Silas high up in glory!"

"Uncle John, I've often heard and read of Andersonville, Georgia, where so many Union soldiers were imprisoned during the war. I've been informed that blood-hounds were kept to chase the prisoners who escaped the stockade."

"Yes, madam; I know a man near this place now that came from Georgia about four years ago, and he lived somewhere near Andersonville in the time of the war. Madam, that man would make you cry if you could hear him tell how the white people used to make the blood-hounds chase the Yankees at that stockade in Andersonville, Georgia. He told me they had blood-hounds all around Andersonville."

"Uncle John, what is the man's name?"

"He is named Samson Jones. Madam, Samson said they had a big dog-kennel where they kept the dogs to chase the Yankees. They run them all through the woods whenever one escaped from the stockade. He told me he had seen many Yankees bitten almost to death by the blood-hounds. He said they used to get out of the stockade and run just like we poor darkies did, with the dogs right behind them. He said the Yankees died like flies in prison, and that he was one of the colored men that helped to bury them there."

"Brother Samson is from Georgia, and he knows all about the Andersonville stockade. So I suppose that his account of the stockade is certainly true?"

"Yes, madam, I believe he is reliable. He told me the wagons used to run night and day burying the prisoners in the warm season. I tell you, madam, Samson could talk all day to you about what he has seen in that stockade at Andersonville, Georgia. He told me thousands of Yankees were walled up in the stockade made of pine-trees, and they had no shed over them. The hot sun used to almost parch them. The rain would pour down on them, and they were shut up like cows in a pasture."

"I've said already, Uncle John, I've read of the horrors of Andersonville; but how strange that these things should be in the State of Georgia, where religion abounds, and where the Gospel was preached Sunday after Sunday, within hearing, perhaps, of the stockade, and that thousands of human souls should receive such brutal treatment!"

They were reduced to a level with the brutes, the barren earth for a floor and the sky their only covering overhead! Samson said the white women used to visit the stockade. They had a platform made so they could walk out and look over the stockade down on the prisoners; and one time a white woman said, when she was looking over at them, "I wish God would rain fire and brimstone down on your heads." Samson said he heard her say it to the Yankees. There they were, dumb and helpless, some dead, some dying, and others almost starved to death. And a Christian woman, so called, cried out to them, "I wish God would rain fire and brimstone down on your heads!" My Lord and my God, we prostrate ourselves before thee and cry, Where are we? In a Christian land? O, that bloody spot, Andersonville! Thy name shall never be erased from the annals of history. The thirteen thousand and seven hundred souls that are now sleeping beneath thy sod, and the hundreds of others that perished in the swamps that surround thee, will rise up in the judgment and condemn thee. Let us thank God and sing:

> "Shout, for the foe is destroyed that inclosed thee,
> The oppressor is vanquished, and Zion is free!"

Not only the bloody ground at Andersonville will condemn the Christians in these Southern States in the general judgment, but what must we say of the millions of poor, innocent slaves that have been murdered here in this Christian land for two hundred and fifty years! "Their blood be upon you and your children!" "Cry aloud, spare not, lift up thy voice like a trumpet, and show my people their transgression, and the house of Jacob their sins."

CHAPTER XII

SALLIE SMITH'S STORY

Sallie Smith living in the woods—Death of her mother—The ill-treatment she suffered.

THE subject of this sketch is another faithful sister of Aunt Charlotte's church. She was born in the State of Louisiana, on Bayou Bœuf. As I had the pleasure of meeting her very often, and, seeing she manifested much interest and real devotion for her church, I became much attached to her. So once as she passed I asked her, if it was not unpleasant to her, if she would please spend a while with me and tell the story of her life as a slave.

She readily assented, saying: "Yes, my dear child. There aint a day but what I think how good my blessed Jesus has been to me and all of my people. O, sometimes I think of my old slave-days, and begin to cry for joy when I remember how good the Lord has been to me. Well do I remember when my poor mother died and left me and my little brother. She called us as she was about to die, and said, 'My dear children, I am going to leave you. The angels is waiting for me. I am almost over. Promise me you will follow me.' I said, 'Mother, is you going to leave us?' and before she could answer she was dead. Madam, I cried night and day; it seemed my mother's death would nearly kill me. We was slaves, and had nobody to care any thing for us. We both had to work hard just like the others on the place. I was about fourteen, and my brother about one year old. The overseer got mad whenever he saw me cry. He told me to hush crying, and said, 'Your mother is dead and in hell, and could not come back here; and if you don't hush I'll beat you half to death.' He was a

Catholic, and hated my mother's sort of religion. When he said my mother was in hell that made me cry more; and he beat me and kicked me all 'round in the field. I had to pick one hundred and fifty pounds of cotton every day or get a whipping at night."

"Were you always able to get one hundred and fifty pounds every day?"

"No, my child, I could not. Sometimes I'd pick it, but I could not get it every day. One night I got up just before day and run away; and I tell you I stayed in the woods one half of my time. Sometimes I'd go so far off from the plantation I could not hear the cows low or the roosters crow."

"Where did you sleep at night, and how did you get something to eat?"

"I slept on logs. I had moss for a pillow; and I tell you, child, I wasn't scared of nothing. I could hear bears, wild-cats, panthers, and every thing. I would come across all kinds of snakes— moccasin, blue runner, and rattlesnakes—and got used to them. One night while I was in the woods a mighty storm came up; the winds blowed, the rain poured down, the hail fell, the trees was torn up by the roots, and broken limbs fell in every direction; but not a hair on my head was injured, but I got as wet as a drowned rat. Next day was a beautiful Sunday, and I dried myself like a buzzard."

"Aunt Sallie, you did not tell me how you got your meals."

"O, child, sometimes I did not get any; but many time I'd find out where the hands on the place were working, and if the overseer was away I'd get something from them. They would bring me something, too, after they found out where I was, and I'd wait on the edge of the woods every day; and when they would come to hunt for me they called out in a low, piercing sound, 'Sallie, Sallie!' I'd come running, and sometimes I was nearly perished."

"Why, Aunt Sallie, it seems to me it was far better for you to have stayed at home than to wander about in the woods."

"No, I could not stay after my mother died. The overseer was mean to me. He beat me every day, and I had no kin on the plantation but my brother, and he could do nothing for me. I got used to staying in the woods, and felt satisfied there. I had a flint-rock and piece of steel, and I could begin a fire any time I wanted. Sometimes I'd get a chicken and would broil it on the coals and would bake ash-cake.

"I remember one night," said Aunt Sallie, "I went to the quarters and knocked at the door of one old lady that belonged to my marster, and she let me in. I asked her for something to eat, but she said, 'I aint got a piece of bread done, but if you want you can bake you a corn-cake.' And bless your soul, child, just as I was about to cook my bread the overseer came in and caught me. La, me! I thought I'd faint when he came in the door."

"Well, what did he do with you?"

"He tied me with a rope by both arms and carried me to the smoke-house. When he got in he throwed the rope over the joist of the smoke-house and left me there all night. He just allowed my toes to touch the floor when he tied me up by my wrists. But, my child, the Lord was with me that night! I managed to get my wrists out of the rope and I sat up nodding in the smoke-house all that night. I was afraid to let him see me down, so just as he was about to unlock the door the next day I slipped my hands back in the rope. He thought I had been tied all night; but, bless the Lord! I was just like Paul and Silas when they were in jail. I cried to the Lord and he loosened the rope. Madam, although I did not have religion when I used to live in the woods, yet it seemed I could not keep from praying. I'd think of my mother, how, just before she died, she told me to 'come.' And that word always followed me. I used to lie out in the woods on the logs, with moss under my head, and pray a many and many a night. I hardly knowed what to say or how to pray, but I remembered how I used to hear my mother praying, on her knees, in the morning before day, long before she died, and I just tried to say what she used to say in her prayers. I heard her say many a time, 'O, Daniel's God, look down from heaven on me, a poor, needy soul!' I would say, 'O, Daniel's God, look down from heaven on me in these woods!' Sometimes it seemed I could see my mother right by my side as I laid on the log asleep. One time I talked with her in my sleep. I asked her, 'Mother, are you well?' And it seemed I could hear her saying, as she beckoned to me,

'Come, O come; will you come?' And I did try to get up in my
sleep and start to her, and I rolled off the log. By that time I
woke up, and the sun was shining clear and bright and I was
there to wander about in the woods?"

"You have not told me what he did with you when he took you
out of the smoke-house that morning."

"Why, he had a big barrel he kept to roll us in, with nails drove
all through it, and he put me in it and had a man to roll me all
over the yard. Madam, I thought he was going to kill me. When
the overseer had me taken out of that barrel I could hardly walk.
I was sore and bruised all over. That night a poor old woman on
our place greased me all over, and I got over with the bruises
and went to work."

"Well, I suppose that was an end to your stay in the woods?"

"No, madam, I did not stay more than a month before I ran
away again. I tell you, I could not stay there. I had got used to
the woods, and the overseer was so brutal to me. The weather
was beginning to turn cold, and I made me a moss bed just like
a hog, and I kept warm at night. But many times I used to sleep
in the chimney-corners on a plantation next to my marster's. I
could hear the colored people inside the cabins pray and sing at
night."

"Why, it seems you could have gone inside the cabins and
stayed with them, Aunt Sallie?"

"Well, yes, I did go in often, but they finally told me I must
stop coming. They said the overseer on their place would beat
them to death if he caught me in their cabins. So I stopped
going inside. They did not know I was outside of the chimney. I
heard them sing many times this hymn:

> "'In the morning when I rise,
> In the morning when I rise,
> In the morning when I rise,
> Give me Jesus, give me Jesus,
> Give me Jesus!
> You may have all this world;
> Give me Jesus!'"

CHAPTER XIII

IN THE WOODS

Aunt Sallie's cruel treatment, continued—Her brother Warren runs away and joins her in the woods.

"THE next time I ran away I met my brother, who had run away two or three weeks before the overseer caught me that night. He told me the overseer beat him so much he could not work. Because I ran away he said my brother knew where I was. My brother's name is Warren. Poor Warren! when he met me that morning he was scarred all over. The overseer told him he had to find me or he would almost skin him. So Warren left the place; but I hadn't seen him in two months, I reckon, till I met him that morning. We sat all day long talking over what we had better do. Warren said, 'Sallie, let me tell you what's best for us to do. You know old Uncle Tim says he can houdoo and make the white folks stop doing us so bad, and let us do what he told us. Let us get some of the white folks' hair and some salt and a piece of old mistress's dress, and make a little bag and sew it up and put it under the steps where all the white folks have to pass over every day. Uncle Tim says it will make the white folks stop treating us so bad. He says when we go to put it under the steps we must say as we throw it, 'Malumbia, Malumbia, peace I want, and peace I must have, in the name of the Lord.'"

"Aunt Sallie, what does Malumbia mean?"

"La, madam, I don't know what it meant. But Warren wanted me to fix the bag and put it under them white folks' steps, but I thought it best to stay in the woods."

"Who is Uncle Tim?"

"He was an old man that stayed around the yard to wait on the

white folks and take care of the horses and cow. He first came
from Africa. He said he used to eat folks in Africa. He could not
talk good like we all could. He came from South Carolina to
Louisiana, when my marster bought him. Uncle Tim had religion, and I used to hear him say, when he would be talking to
my mother, 'Me lover my Lord like my Lord lover me; me *never
eater poor soul* no more.' I don't even remember when he came
to Louisiana. It was long before I was born; but I heard people
say he was right from Africa to this country. We all used to call
him 'Uncle Summer-time' and he liked that name. He was a
good old man, but he believed in houdoo. O, yes; no doubt they
were heathen habits that he learned in his native land. I used to
hear him many times, when he would be down on his knees
praying, say, 'O, Shadrach, Meshach, Abed-Negroes' God
blesses poor Summer-time's soul!' and then he would stop still
and holler out, 'O, how me loves my Lord like my Lord loves
me!' Although I was young I will never forget Uncle Tim
Summer-time."

"Aunt Sallie, what did you and your brother decide upon in
the woods!"

"O, we wandered about in the woods, I don't know how long.
We would pick berries to eat, and would get any thing we came
upon. I told Warren about my dream of our mother, and that I
saw her come up to me, and that I had been praying every night
on my moss bed. I wanted to get him to pray too. I said to him,
'Warren, you know how our poor mother used to pray way
before day in the morning, and how we used to hear her cry and
say, "O, Daniel's God, have mercy on me!" And it makes me feel
glad every time I pray, Warren; and now let us pray every time
before we go to sleep.' Warren said, 'Well, let us pray to Daniel's
God just like our poor mother did.' And we did every night
before we went to sleep, after wandering all through the woods
all day. Me and Warren would pray. We prayed low and easy; we
just could hear each other. Warren used to pray, 'O, Daniel's
God, have mercy on me and Sallie. Mother said you will take
care of us, but we suffer here; nobody to help us. Hear us way
up in heaven and look down on us here.' Madam, we did not

know hardly what to say, but we had heard mother and other people praying, and we tried to do the best we could. Sometimes we was so hungry we could hardly sleep, and it would be so cold, too, we did not know what to do. We had a big heap of moss, and we made a brush arbor over it to keep the rain off. I took Warren to the same place where I had been going at night in the chimney-corners to keep warm. But, la, madam, one morning we overslept ourselves and the overseer of that plantation caught us. He carried us home to old mistress. I heard her tell old marster to not to let the overseer hit us a lick. She said, 'Send them to the kitchen and give them a plenty to eat and stop whipping them, and see if you can't do more with them.' Madam, I tell you when I overheard her talking to marster tears came in my eyes. I told Warren. O, how glad we felt that morning! I cried for joy.

"After they gave us something to eat they let us rest awhile. Me and Warren went to our house and we talked how mistress looked like she was sorry for us when she saw us just come out of the woods that morning. We hardly ever saw her, for we lived in quarters and the house was away off. I told Warren Daniel's God had heard us praying in the woods, and I said, 'Warren, let us keep on praying and trusting in God.' I said, 'You know the overseer used to beat us whenever he caught us, and roll me in the barrel, tie me up by my waist-band, and punish us all sorts of ways.' But this morning he got us and did not give us a lick, but gave us a good breakfast and sent us out here to rest. Madam, me and Warren agreed right there not to give up praying night and day. We did follow our mother's rule. We would get up long before time to go to work to pray."

"So, Aunt Sallie, you did not believe in voudous?"

"No, ma'am. The next time I saw Uncle Tim I told him I did not believe in it. I said, 'Uncle Tim, I have been praying ever since my mother died, and you see the overseer don't do me as he used to. I tell you, Uncle Tim, Daniel's God heard me and Warren.' He told us to keep on praying; said, 'Daniel's God is a great God. He will hear his children when they cry.' He was a good old man, but we could not understand him much what he said, and he believed in houdoos."

"Yes, the vice of voudouism which is practiced among the colored people is the result of ignorance and slavery. They will, in the course of time, ignore such doctrine, for they are being educated, and the time will come when such simple and nonsensical teachings will find no place among them."

"Yes, ma'am; I believe they will learn better in the course of time."

"Well, tell me, Aunt Sallie, did you both finally remain at home after you were caught in the chimney-corner?"

"Yes, ma'am; we stayed after that. The overseer stopped doing us bad; but we had to work mighty hard to keep up. We both was blessed to see freedom. My brother is living right now in Springtown, and he comes to see me every Christmas. We both are soldiers for Jesus. He is a deacon in a Baptist church, and I am one of your noisy dry-land Methodists."

CHAPTER XIV

UNCLE STEPHEN JORDON

Uncle Stephen sold with a calf—A sheriff's sale in slave-days—He is
made to leave his wife and children, and is given another by his
master—He does not want the new one.

ONE of the most interesting persons I ever conversed with
about his history as a slave was Uncle Stephen Jordon. I
had heard so much of his remarkable career as a slave that I
made up my mind that the very next time I met him I would get
him to give me a sort of a sketch of his life as a slave. So one day,
as I sat on my front gallery, when he was about to pass my house,
I called him in. Said I:

"Uncle Stephen, I've heard so much of your remarkable experience as a slave that I thought the very next chance I got I
would ask you to relate to me the history of your slave-life. Will
you not favor me by so doing? I've heard Aunt Charlotte's, Aunt
Lorendo's, Uncle John's, and many others; but I've been told so
much about your history that I have long craved to have you
recite it yourself."

"Well, madam," said he, "I assure you that my history has been
a wonderful one. I tell you, my dear child, nobody but God knows
the trouble we poor black folks had to undergo in slave-time.
My first old master was a mighty good man, and my mistress
used to love me like her own children. In fact, my old master
was my own father; but, of course, the thing was kept a sort of a
secret, although every body knew it. My mother was one of the
house servants, and I was raised about the white folks' house.
Indeed, after I was old enough to be weaned old mistress had
me to sleep in a couch with her own children in her own room,

until I got to be a great big boy. The children and I used to play together, and after they began to go to school I used to go with them to carry their books and lunch, and they taught me every lesson they learned, so that when I was about fourteen or fifteen years old I could read and write as well as any of them. But I tell you, child, this thing did not last forever. Somehow or other old master got broke, and his big plantation and all his slaves were seized and sold for debts. This was in the parish of ——, in the State of Louisiana. I can never forget the day of that sale. I had never seen an auction sale before, although I had often heard of it. The sale had been widely advertised; and on that day rich planters from all along the coast and some merchants and others from New Orleans, who wanted house servants or other help for their stores, were there in large numbers. As soon as every thing was ready, exactly at twelve o'clock—I remember it as well as if it was yesterday—the drum began to tap and every body followed it to the old sugar-house shed, where the sale was to take place. When every body had gathered, the slaves, numbering about two hundred and fifty head, counting men, women, and children, were all put together on one side; and all the wagons, teams, horses, cows, calves, and other cattle on another; and the buyers were all in front of the auction-block. So soon as every thing was ready the sheriff got on the old sugar-house cane-carrier and began the sale. He first read from a newspaper the decree of the court under which the sale was to take place; and then he described the property to be sold, including the plantation, wagons, mules, cattle, and all the slaves. After he had sold the plantation, wagons, mules, horses, and cattle he began to sell the slaves. Some were bought by neighboring planters, some by the merchants and others that had come from New Orleans, and others were bought by negro traders to be placed in the market and sold again. My mother was bought by one of the New Orleans merchants; but I was bought by a negro trader. My old mistress was sorry to part with me and a little pet calf she had raised around the big house. So she had us kept until the last to see if she could not keep us; but old master's debts could not be met after every thing else had been sold, so the calf and

I had to be sold. The negro trader bought me and the calf together for five hundred and thirty dollars. Next day all of us who had been sold to buyers living in and along the coast toward New Orleans were shipped on a steam-boat going that way. My mother was on that boat. That night we reached New Orleans. Mother was taken to her new owner's house to be a house servant, and I was taken to the arcade, or negro traders' yard. From that day until peace was declared after the war I never laid my eyes on my dear mother; that was nearly twenty years. I tell you, people were miserable in that old slave-pen. Every day buyers came and examined such slaves as they desired to buy. They used to make them open their mouths so that they could examine their teeth; and they used to strip them naked, from head to foot, to see whether they were perfectly sound. And this they did to women as well as men. I tell you, my dear child, it used to seem to me so brutal to see poor women treated in that way by brutal and heartless men. I declare, child, I can't understand it, although I've been right in it. When they would put them naked that way they used to switch them on the legs to make them jump around so that buyers could see how supple they were."

"I declare, Uncle Stephen, your story makes me shudder."

"It was so, just as I tell you; but I did not stay long in the negro traders' yard. I was sold soon after that to a man that lived only a few miles from the old place where I was raised and sold from when mother and I was separated. My new master was a mighty mean man, and would not allow any of his slaves to go anywhere. He notified all the 'poor 'Cadien patrollers' to whip his slaves whenever they caught any of them off the place."

"Who were these 'Cadien patrollers, Uncle Stephen?"

"Why, child, they were the meanest things in creation; they were poor, low down white folks, that descended from a French and Spanish mixture. They had no slaves themselves, and so they just took pleasure in patrolling the public roads so as to get to whip somebody else's slaves that happened to be out without a pass."

"I had often heard that before; but I just asked you to see whether what I had heard of them was true."

"It is just so, child. They were a poor, ignorant set that was just as mean as they were poor and ignorant. The only advantage they had over the negroes was that they were white, that's all. Well, as I was going to tell you, master would not allow his slaves to go off the place. In order to keep them on the place he used to give them wives right on the place. He would not allow his slaves to take wives that did not belong to his plantation. Whenever he thought one of his men needed a wife or one of his women needed a husband he would choose them and put them together. If he did not own them he would go and buy a wife or a husband for those that he thought were old enough and needed them. He would never allow the men to be single after they were eighteen, nor the women after they were fifteen. I remember one day, when he had returned from town with about twenty-five heads of slaves, he called out all those who had no wives or husbands on the place. Said he, 'Well, boys, I've gotten a fine set of girls for you, and I am going to put you all together; likewise you, girls, I've got these fine boys, and I am going to put you all together, so that there will be no reason for any of you to have wives and husbands off the place. That old practice has got to stop'; so then he gave each one his wife or husband; he chose them out himself."

"Did he give you one, too, Uncle Stephen?"

"Why, yes, child, he gave me mine, too."

"What did you say?"

"Well, what could I say, but take her and go along? But I tell you, child, there was great sorrow on the place that day. Many of us had wives or husbands on neighboring plantations; I myself had my wife on another plantation. The woman my master gave me had a husband on another plantation. Every thing was mixed up. My other wife had two children for me, but the woman master gave me had no children. We were put in the same cabin, but both of us cried, me for my old wife and she for her old husband. As I could read and write I used to write out passes for myself, so I could go and see my old wife; and I wrote passes for the other men on the place, so they could go and see their wives that lived off the place."

CHAPTER XV

COUNTERFEIT FREE PAPERS

The overseer searches Uncle Stephen's cabin and finds his counterfeit free papers—His master about to kill him, but finally determines to sell him—Uncle Stephen's new master—His break for freedom and capture—His sentence to be hanged, and his freedom finally.

"UNCLE Stephen, what did you do with the wife your master gave you?"

"Well, we stayed in the same cabin together, not as husband and wife, but as son and mother, she was so much older than I; and I used to write out passes and slip them to her husband that lived on a neighboring plantation, so he could come and see her. But I tell you, child, things got to be so tight that I could not get to see my wife as often as I wanted; so I made up my mind to run away. There was an old free negro that lived near our place; I got him to let me see his free papers. I tell you, child, I took those free papers and copied every word of them. 'Now,' said I, 'I shall run away, and if I am caught I shall show these counterfeit free papers and get off all right.' Sure enough, I took those papers and stowed them away in a secret place in my cabin, together with my mother's picture and my own picture, which was taken when we belonged to Mr. Jordon, my first old master, together with some old passes, books, and papers. But one day, I don't know why, he suspected me. One of our slaves ran away, and the overseer was hunting for him. The overseer hunted every-where for him. While hunting for that runaway he went and searched my cabin; finally he found my papers. When I found out that the overseer had found my papers and turned them over to my master I just made up my mind that I certainly would be killed. I tell you, child, the very thought makes my blood chill even now. It seemed like the news had gone out like wild-fire through the quarters that passes, free papers, and books had been found in 'poor Stephen's house,' and that old master was going to kill him. I had no sooner reached the big gate where I had gone to put up my mules in the stable than I heard the overseer cry out:

"'Ah, Stephen! your master is waiting for you at the big house; never mind about your mules, but go right out to the house, where he will make an eternal settlement with you.'

"'There now,' said I, 'I am gone.' As I stepped on the porch of the big house I saw old master sitting in his dining-room with a table before him. On the table were all of my letters, old passes, free papers, newspapers, books, and other papers, and by the side of these old master had a fearful-looking dagger and two army revolvers.

"'Ah,' said he, 'you are the one that gives passes to my niggers and makes free papers for those who run away.' And he swore at me.

"I tried to answer, but he was in such a rage he would hear nothing. I thought he would kill me every minute. Finally he said:

"'Who taught you how to write? I did not know you were educated. Here you are, better educated than any white man around here. An educated nigger is a dangerous thing, and the best place for him is six feet under the ground, buried face foremost. Ah, sir, your end is come, and you will not have use for papers, books, and pens any longer.'

"I tell you, madam, I just made up my mind that my time had come and I would surely die. At last old master quieted a little, and I said:

"'Master, I was raised in the house, and Master Jordon's children taught me how to read and write. But,' said I, 'I never wrote a free paper for any body in my life. True, I wrote those counterfeit free papers and put the name Sam in it, calling myself by that false name so that I might run away, because I could not get to see my old wife and children that live on Mr. François's place, but, master, I declare I never wrote free papers for any body in my life.'

"Of course I had written out the passes for the other slaves, but, although I knew it was a sin, to save myself I had to say that I just wrote the passes for pastime. How that man did not kill me I can't imagine, excepting that God would not let him. So he says to me:

"'Your old master, Jordon, is to blame for this crime, and he ought to pay for it. That's the reason he is broke and don't own a dollar to-day; but you can't stay here to spoil all my niggers; you can't stay here another week.'

"I tell you, child, you can't imagine how glad I was to get off so easy. I remained on that place only two days after that, and then a Mr. Valsin, that kept a big store, bought me to work in his store.

"Mr. Valsin, my new master, seemed to be ever so well pleased with me. His store was in a thick settlement about fifteen miles up the Mississippi River above my last master's plantation. I did all the work around the store, and, as I was good at figuring and could read and write, he had me to weigh out things and to wait on many of the customers whenever he needed me. I liked him very well, and I took great interest in his business. Mr. Valsin had a fair-sized plantation in connection with his store, and owned about fifty head of slaves. Generally he was a good man, but when angry he was of a very violent temper. That is where I was living about the time that the late civil war began and when New Orleans fell into the hands of the Union soldiers. But being about twenty miles from where my wife was living, and not being able to see or hear from her for several years, I finally had to give up the hope of ever seeing her again, and so I took up with another woman that lived on our place. About the time that General Butler captured New Orleans slaves were running into the Union line from all around our neighborhood. So one day Mr. Valsin says to me,

"'Well, Stephen, I suppose you will do like some of the other niggers, and run away from me.'

"'No, indeed,' said I, 'I shall never leave you. Those Yankees are too bad, I hear.'

"'That's so,' he said; 'you will do much better to stay with me and run off with us to Texas before they get here.'

"Of course I liked Mr. Valsin well enough, but I rather be free than be with him, or be the slave of any body else. So his word about going to Texas rather sunk deep into me, because I was praying for the Yankees to come up our way just as soon as possible. I dreaded going to Texas, because I feared that I would never get free. The same thought was in the mind of every one of the slaves on our place. So two nights before we were to leave for Texas all the slaves on our place had a secret meeting at midnight, when we decided to leave to meet the Yankees. Sure enough, about one o'clock that night every one of us took through the woods to make for the Union line. The moon was shining like day. After we had traveled till about four o'clock in the morning, the way through the woods being rather rough, we took the public road next to the river. We suddenly came where the levee made a short and sudden bend. The water in the river was up to the bank, and on the other side was a very high fence. In that yard were several bad dogs. While here, all at once before us we heard about a dozen men on horseback. They came right on us, and cried out, 'Halt! halt!' Several jumped the fence and made for the woods, while the dogs almost devoured them; but twenty-five of us were captured by this band. We hoped that they were advanced guards of Union soldiers, but instead of that they proved to be 'Cadien patrollers watching out for runaways. I tell you, child, we were in a bad fix. We were all handcuffed, two by two, and a chain was passed between us linking all the handcuffs, and we were marched back to our master. Mr. Valsin was so mad he wanted to kill us all. He then charged me with planning for all who had previously run away. Some mercy was to be shown to the others, but I was the educated one; I was the one that had planned all this devilment, as he called it, and I was to be killed as an example for all the rest. For this I was sent away out to New Iberia, where I was placed in jail preparatory to my execution. Then the Yankees were coming so fast they decided to send me to Opelousas jail, where I was finally to suffer death for conspiring and assisting slaves to escape. While in this jail I waited every day for the time when I was to be hung until I was pronounced dead. The scaffold was built just outside the jail, and next day at twelve o'clock I was to die on that scaffold. But that very night, by some means or other that I've never been fully able to understand, I was bought by a man that lived in Texas. He, with the jailer, woke me up and took me out, and I was that very night shipped off to Texas, where I remained until the war was over and peace was declared. My Texas master, Mr. Maxwell, treated me very kindly, and when the war was over he told me that I was my own free man, and could go or stay just as I thought best. As he was a very clever kind of a man I contracted with him and worked for him one year, after which I returned to the city of New Orleans, where I was reunited to my mother and my present wife, whom I married at Mr. Valsin's. My other wife had married, as I had also done during the long years of our enforced and hopeless separation. The children I had with her are now grown and have entered upon the active duties of life. Since that I have accumulated property and have done some good, I hope, in the world, and am now enjoying a happy and contented old age.

"But I tell you, child, I was fortunate to find my mother, my wife, and my children. So many who were separated by slavery were never reunited again in this world, and will never meet again until they enter the eternal world."

"That's very true," said I; "but, Uncle Stephen, haven't you heard of that wonderful column in the *South-western Christian Advocate* called the 'Lost Friends' Column?' By means of an advertisement in that column I have heard of friends and relatives that long had been separated being brought together. Why, I suppose my husband could tell you of several hundreds of such cases. One told me the other day of her relatives whom she had left in West Virginia years before the war; another of her relatives in South Carolina, whom they had found by advertising in that column. So I have heard of others, whose relatives had been left in Virginia, Maryland, Kentucky, Tennessee, Georgia, Mississippi, Texas, and, in fact, in every Southern and other States, that thus have been restored to each other. I tell you, these reunions must be seasons of great joy. I don't suppose there's any thing like it except the glorious reunion in our Father's house when life and its cares are all over!"

CHAPTER XVI

UNCLE CEPHAS'S STORY

Lizzie Beaufort would rather die than live a wicked life—Her brother
Cato runs away, hides in the swamps, and finally makes his way to
freedom by the aid of the Underground Railroad—Cato becomes
a soldier, senator, and congressman—How Uncle Cephas learned
to read, bought himself, and became a rich and honored citizen.

MY interest in, and conversations with, Aunt Charlotte, Aunt
Sallie, Uncle John Goodwin, Uncle Stephen, and the other
characters represented in this story led me to interview many
other people that could give me any additional facts and inci-
dents about the colored people, in freedom as well as in slavery.

Uncle Cephas, who used to live in Tennessee before the war,
and who came to Louisiana at the close of the late war of the
rebellion, told me many things which I am sure would interest
any one. He told me a very pathetic story of a colored girl, eighteen years old, whose master had bought her in South Carolina
and brought her to Tennessee. Her name was Lizzie Beaufort.
She was a most beautiful girl. She had large black eyes, long
black hair, a beautiful oval-shaped face, and was of a fine oily
brunette complexion. She might have easily passed for a Cuban;
but she was the slave of her own father, who had sold her to this
Tennessee planter. Her Tennessee master had bought her to be
his kept woman, but Lizzie declared that she would rather die a
thousand deaths than live such a life. She was willing to work
her hands off, and do any thing that was required of her, but she
just told her master that he would have her to kill, but that she
never would submit to be made the instrument of his hateful
lust. It was of no use. He coaxed, he pleaded, he threatened, and

he beat her, but Lizzie stood as firmly as a rock against all his advances.

When he saw that he could not persuade her by any means he determined to sell her. She was sold to a negro trader, who brought her out to Mississippi.

Uncle Cephas told me also the story of Lizzie's brother, Cato, who made his way from the rice-fields of South Carolina to Canada about ten years before the war. Uncle Cephas got the facts from Lizzie's own lips.

He said: "Lizzie told me all about it herself. Cato ran away and was gone over two months before they knew what had become of him. It took him all that time dodging in the swamps until he could make his way through the free States into Canada. But after he got to Canada he wrote back to a friendly white man that lived in the neighborhood, who told Lizzie and her mother all about it. The white man was from the North, and was very friendly to us colored people, but he had to be mighty careful about showing it, because all the white people suspicioned him, because they said he was a Northern man. He was the one that helped Cato to make his escape. It was good that he was not found out, for they certainly would have killed him. He bargained with a ship-master to take Cato from Charleston to Boston. Cato was packed in a box and shipped for a box of cabbage. He was packed in the box with cabbage-leaves all around him, to make the box appear as a box of cabbage sure enough. The white man was an agent of what was then known as the Underground Railroad. He notified the Underground Railroad people in Boston of the time when Cato would reach Boston, so that they might get him and run him off into Canada before he should be captured, if discovered, under the Fugitive Slave Act, which was then in force all over this country.

"The Lord was with Cato, however, and he reached Canada in safety. He fell in among good people there, and was soon doing well. He soon got a good education and plenty of property. When the war broke out he came back to Boston, joined the Union army, and came South and fought in some of the hardest battles of the war. A cousin of mine, who used to know

Lizzie in Tennessee, met her near Vicksburg two years ago, and she told him that Cato was then living there, and was one of the greatest leaders of his race in Mississippi. He had been sheriff of his county, had been a senator, and had served his State in Congress and in several other stations of honor and trust."

"But," said I, "Uncle Cephas, you speak very properly for one that was a slave. You must have got an education notwithstanding the law against negroes being permitted to learn how to read and write."

"Ah, my child," said he, "my life has been an eventful one. It is true that slaves were not permitted to learn how to read; but I was determined to learn if it was any way possible to do so. You see I was not born free, but my master and his wife died when I was only five years old. They were old people, and had no children; so they left me and all my relatives free in their will. Notwithstanding that, however, the will was contested in court and found defective, and we were all sold to satisfy claims against the estate. Mother was sold to a man that lived in Alabama, brother Jerry to one that lived in North Carolina, and sister Rachel to a negro trader that sold her to a family in Florida. I was sold to judge S——, in Tennessee. He was one of the most heartless men that ever lived. I can't begin to tell you of his meanness. I suppose if I had lived with him till the emancipation I would never have amounted to any thing, but, as the Lord would have it, he got broke by his senseless extravagance and was sold out at sheriff sale, and in that sale I was bought by Parson Winslow, a very kind-hearted old Methodist preacher. Parson told me that he did not buy me because he needed any slaves, but because he thought I had too good a turn to be made a dog of by such a heartless master. Parson Winslow knew me well, because whenever he came on his circuit in our neighborhood and stopped at our house I had to take care of his horse for him. After I had stayed with him about ten years one day he said to me: 'Cephas, I see you are a mighty smart boy, and seem to be making extra dimes by doing odd jobs around. I want to encourage your manly disposition. I want to fix it so you can buy yourself, your wife, and your children. What do you say to that?'

"Why, madam, that word went through me like lightning. I had saved some money for that very purpose, but never dared propose the matter to the parson. (We never called him any thing but parson. He wouldn't let us call him any thing else.) So as soon as he made the proposition I gladly accepted the offer.

"'But,' said I, 'parson, I'll never be able to pay you for myself, my wife, and my children. How can I?' 'Well,' said he, 'pay me twenty-five dollars a month for your time, and whatever you make over that shall be yours.' I had a very good trade; I was a blacksmith and machinist, and I could get two dollars and a half a day for every working-day in the year. I told Dinah, my wife, all about it, and she was perfectly delighted. From that on I worked and Dinah worked. We both worked, and I tell you, madam, before many more years passed over my head I had bought myself, Dinah, and our two children.

"All the years I was at the parson's I was never without a book or paper about me. His children used to teach me on the sly when they came to see Dinah. Dinah was the cook, and a mighty good one she was, too. After I was free I just made good for lost time and learned all I could, so that when the war came on I was a pretty good scholar. I was not satisfied to see myself free and make no efforts to help others of my race. Having such a good trade and a plenty of work I made plenty of money and saved it. Dinah, too, was a very smart woman. So by her help and the help of our two boys we could always lay our hands on several hundred dollars in hard cash. With that I bought poor slaves, I can scarcely tell you how many. I would buy them and then give them time to pay me. When they worked and paid me what I paid for them I would give them their free papers. Let's see, I did that for Jim Sanders, who was a very smart man, and who after the war became Secretary of State in his adopted State; for Frank Shorter, who became a member of Congress, and a number of others. These, however, were exceptionally brilliant men, and lost no time in pushing themselves right to the front. Jim, I believe, is still a senator, and has been in one branch or another of the Legislature of his State for the last twenty years. Of course I can't help from calling them Jim and Frank, I know them so well. Jim lives in Louisiana, and Frank lives in South

Carolina. In fact, every one I helped in that way proved to be of the best metal. Nearly all of them were active in the reconstruction of their States, were in the constitutional conventions, the legislatures, etc.; and but for the suppression of negro majorities in the South I suppose many of them would still be felt as great political agencies in this country. Several of them, however, like myself, are growing old, and are leading a quiet home-life; and then others of them have died and gone the way of all the earth. I never cared about politics myself, however. I never thought our salvation depended so much upon politics. Education, property, and character, to my mind, have ever been the trinity of power to which I have looked and do look for our complete redemption in this country. No earthly power can undermine and destroy the progress of a people thus intrenched. With that principle in me, I have ever tried to regulate my practice accordingly. I educated both of my sons and gave them each a good trade. One of them, however, is now a physician in Texas, and the other is pastor of one of the largest churches in Washington, D. C. He graduated with high honors at one of the best theological schools in this country, and is to-day a recognized authority in Greek, Hebrew, and the Shemitic languages. They are both good boys, and Dinah and I are proud of them. I like to recall and talk over such matters; they stir up all the enthusiasm of my younger days."

It would have done you good to have heard Uncle Cephas tell his story. Although he is now an old man, he is yet so vigorous and pressed in the business of his blacksmith shop, which he still runs with hired workmen, that I could no longer detain him, and had to bid him good-bye, with the request that he call again. He is one of our most substantial citizens, and is assessed at thirty-five thousand dollars, most of which is in lands and city property well and desirably located.

CHAPTER XVII

A COLORED SOLDIER

Colonel Douglass Wilson on the war—Color-bearer Planchiancio and
   Captain Caillioux—Joel Brinkley, a Yankee school-teacher, caned
   nearly to death.

AFTER my conversation with Uncle Cephas in the last chapter
I did not get to see any one particularly for a month or
more who could add materially to my story any thing that might
interest you; but during the succeeding summer, after this last
conversation, I met Colonel Douglass Wilson, a colored man of
considerable prominence, not only in Louisiana, but in the
nation. He and his family and my husband, daughter, and I were
spending a vacation at Bay St. Louis, Mississippi, a very popular
watering-place on the Mississippi Sound. He and my husband
were very great friends, and used to visit each other during our
stay there. One day I said to him:

"Colonel, from what I have heard you say and learned of you
generally, as a public man, you must have a rich experience
touching occurrences before, during, and since the war among
our people. I have made the matter one of deep study, and I
know your story would delight almost any one. Don't keep all
the good things to yourself; tell us about them sometime."

"Yes," said he, "my experience is a rich and varied one, and I
am so constantly telling it every-where and on every occasion
that I fear sometimes that people will say that I have a hobby."

"I assure you," said I, "you will never hear that from me,
because I believe we should not only treasure these things, but
should transmit them to our children's children. That's what the
Lord commanded Israel to do in reference to their deliverance

from Egyptian bondage, and I verily believe that the same is his will concerning us and our bondage and deliverance in this country. After thirty-three centuries the Jews are more faithful in the observance of the facts connected with their bondage and deliverance than we are in those touching ours, although our deliverance took place scarcely a quarter of a century ago."

"You are right, Mrs. Albert," replied the colonel, "and that is my principal reason for so heartily concurring with those of our leading colored men who are doing all in their power to induce all of our people in this country to unite every year in the observance of January 1 as National Emancipation Day. There can be no doubt that that is the day every true American should celebrate as National Emancipation Day, as that was the day on which Mr. Lincoln's ever-memorable proclamation of freedom was issued—January 1, 1863."

"Colonel, let me ask you, were you ever a slave?"

"A slave? Why, yes; I was a slave until Mr. Lincoln's proclamation of freedom. It found me, however, on the battle-field at Port Hudson, La., where the colored troops fought so nobly as to extort from their chief officers such praises as were showered upon few soldiers at any time or place. I was there in the hottest of the fight, when Captain Caillioux, that valiant negro, fell, one whose praises can never be too loudly proclaimed. If ever patriotic heroism deserved to be honored in stately marble or in brass that of Captain Caillioux deserves to be, and the American people will have never redeemed their gratitude to genuine patriotism until that debt is paid. I was there, yes, ma'am, when, with one arm dangling in his sleeve, the brave captain waved his comrades on to the bloody conflict with the other. I was there, too, and heard the lion-hearted color-bearer, Planchiancio, when he received the regimental colors from his superior officer, and, grasping them with a firm and manly hand, assured him that he would 'return with those colors from the sweeping, bloody fray with honor, or report to God the reason why.' The recital of these things fires all the military ardor in my soul. From that day to the close of the war 'Remember Port Hudson' was the talismanic watchword that ever inspired our regiment to the highest degree of heroism. But Port Hudson was only one of a hundred battle-fields whereon the colored soldier demonstrated his valor. There were Fort Pillow, Fort Wagner, Chickamauga, Fort Blakely, Fort Donelson, Lake Providence, Pulaski, Waterproof, Appomattox, and a hundred others. The verdict was that 'the colored troops fought nobly.'

"O, yes, I was a slave, but I became, a soldier, too, and fought for freedom and the Union, and I am proud of it. But I want to tell you that this last war exploded many false notions in the minds of our Southern people, and in some of our Northern neighbors, too. They used to say, 'The negro doesn't care to be set free, and but for Northern meddlers you would never hear any complaints from him.' Then they said, 'If you free him he will die out'; but I tell you he is the liveliest corpse this nation has ever handled. He is multiplying faster than any people in this country. When it was proposed to make a soldier out of him, why, they said, 'He can't fight.' But what was the universal verdict at the close of every battle? Why, he fought like a demon. After the war they said, 'O, he can't learn!' But what mean these laurels that he is getting at Yale, Cornell, Dartmouth, and other colleges over white competitors? Whether he wanted freedom or not is beautifully illustrated in a story that came under my observation.

"Among thousands of contrabands, as they were called, that flocked into the Union lines, as the Yankees captured various sections in the South, were a very aged man and his wife. The slaves were escaping from the old plantations in every direction. So one morning a planter out near Vicksburg, Miss., went out into his negro quarters, and, addressing this aged patriarch, now bent under the weight of over threescore and ten years, said, 'Uncle Si, I don't suppose you are going off to those hateful Yankees, too, are you?' 'O no, marster,' he said, 'I'se gwine to stay right here with you.' Next morning the planter visited the quarters again, when he found that every one of his slaves, not excepting even Uncle Si and his wife, Aunt Cindy, had gone to the Yankees during the night. Searching out in the woods for them, he finally came upon Uncle Si, just inside the Union line.

Aunt Cindy was stretched out on the bare ground, dead, and Uncle Si was bending over her, weeping. She had died from the exposure and hardship incident upon the making of their escape. Addressing Uncle Si, the planter said, 'Uncle Si, why on earth did you so cruelly bring Aunt Cindy here for, through all of such hardship, thereby causing her death?' Lifting up his eyes and looking his master full in the face, he answered, 'I couldn't help it, marster; but then, you see, she died free.'"

"Colonel, tell me something about the Kuklux. Did you know any thing about them? They were said to be very bad and numerous in Georgia and South Carolina."

"That's true; at that time they were very bad and numerous in both Georgia and South Carolina, but they were equally bad in Louisiana, Mississippi, Texas, and, in fact, throughout the South. They were known in some places as the White Camelias, the White Cohort, and other such names, but after all they were nothing more nor less than the Confederate army that had surrendered at Appomattox that was really continuing a sort of guerrilla warfare against Union men and the poor freedmen. This was what made the task of reconstruction such a difficult one throughout the South. The Kuklux were determined that the colored people, if now free, should not enjoy their freedom, but should remain in a condition of peonage. To accomplish their purpose they heaped all sorts of indignities upon the northern white missionary preachers and teachers that followed the march of the Union lines to organize our people in church relations and to establish schools among them. Not only were they socially ostracized, but they were maltreated, whipped, mobbed, and massacred by wholesale.

"I remember, just now, the case of Mr. Joel Brinkley, who was taken out of his school-house, right before his scholars, in broad day-time, and caned half to death by a mob of nearly a hundred of those hyenas. After that they gave him five hours in which to leave the town of Springdale, where he was teaching. After he started off they thought they ought to have killed him, so they started off after him to catch him, and they followed him for ten days, trying to catch him. He had to hide in the swamps, sleep in the cane-rows and ditches and under negro cabins to save his life. A reward of five hundred dollars was offered for his apprehension and delivery into their hands, but the Lord was with him, and he finally reached New Orleans in safety, where he could continue in the same line of work with a little more security. I have often heard him tell of how kindly the colored people treated him when he was then fleeing for his life. They were the only friends he could trust. They would hide him under their cabins and in their hay-lofts, and feed him there until it was safe for him to journey on farther. From them, too, he could learn of the whereabouts of the human hounds that were pursuing him for his life. Mr. Brinkley, however, was fortunate to have gotten away with his life, notwithstanding the fact that he thereby contracted terrible constitutional troubles, from which he suffered many years. Hundreds of others were killed outright, their churches or school-houses burnt down, and their families driven away. They were equally murdered, however, some instantly, while others, like Mr. Brinkley, died a slower death."

CHAPTER XVIII

NEGRO GOVERNMENT

Kuklux—Reign of terror—Black laws—Reconstruction—Colored men in constitutional conventions and State legislatures—Lieutenant-Governor Dunn—Honest Antoine Dubuclet—Negro problem—What the race has accomplished since the war—Emigration and colonization.

"IF the Kuklux treated the missionaries in that manner you must not imagine that they left the colored people and their children unharmed. Thousands of colored men and women throughout the South were in like manner whipped and shot down like dogs, in the fields and in their cabins. The recital of some of the experiences of those days is enough to chill your blood and raise your hair on ends. The horrors of those days can scarcely be imagined by those who know nothing about it. Why, madam, you ought to have been down here in 1868. That was the year in which Grant and Colfax ran for President and Vice-President, against Seymour and Blair. A perfect reign of terror existed all over the South; and the colored people who attempted to vote were shot down like dogs every-where. There was such a reign of terrorism in many States of the South that the Congress of the United States refused to count the bloody electoral votes of several of the Southern States. Two years before that, in July, 1866, there was a constitutional convention in New Orleans, to frame a constitution whereby the State of Louisiana might be reconstructed and re-admitted into the Union. On the 30th day of that month, I believe it was, a fearful riot was instituted by those fire-eaters, and the result was that the streets of New Orleans were flooded with negro blood.

Hundreds of them were killed without any knowledge of the murderous intentions of their enemies. They lay dead on every street and in the gutter, and were taken out and buried in trenches by the cart-load in all the cemeteries. The children at school were also the object of the same murderous spirit. When we sent our children to school in the morning we had no idea that we should see them return home alive in the evening.

"Big white boys and half-grown men used to pelt them with stones and run them down with open knives, both to and from school. Sometimes they came home bruised, stabbed, beaten half to death, and sometimes quite dead. My own son himself was often thus beaten. He has on his forehead to-day a scar over his right eye which sadly tells the story of his trying experience in those days in his efforts to get an education. I was wounded in the war, trying to get my freedom, and he over the eye, trying to get an education. So we both call our scars marks of honor. In addition to these means to keep the negro in the same servile condition. I was about to forget to tell you of the 'black laws,' which were adopted in nearly all of the Southern States under President Andrew Johnson's plan of reconstruction. They adopted laws with reference to contracts, to the movement of negro laborers, etc., such as would have made the condition of the freed negro worse than when he had a master before the war. But, in the words of General Garfield upon the death of President Lincoln, 'God reigns, and the government at Washington still lives.' It did live, and, notwithstanding Andrew Johnson, it lived under the divine supervision which would not and did not allow the Southern States to reconstruct upon any such dishonorable, unjust plan to the two hundred thousand negro soldiers who offered their lives upon the altar for the perpetuation of the Union and the freedom of their country. And the whole matter was repudiated by Congress, and the States were reconstructed upon the plan of equal rights to every citizen, of whatever race or previous condition. It was then declared that, whereas the stars on our national flag had been the property of only the white race and the stripes for only the colored, now the stars should forever be the common property of both, and that the stripes should only be given to those that deserved them.

"Under this new plan of reconstruction many colored men entered the constitutional conventions of every Southern State; and in the subsequent organization of the new State governments colored men took their seats in both branches of the State governments, in both Houses of Congress, and in all the several branches of the municipal, parochial, State, and national governments. It is true that many of them were not prepared for such a radical and instantaneous transition. But I tell you, madam, it was simply wonderful to see how well they did. And although in the midst of prejudice and partisan clamor a great deal of the most withering criticisms have been spent upon the ignorance, venality, and corruption of the negro carpet-bag reconstruction governments inaugurated by our people, I believe time will yet vindicate them, and their achievements will stand out in the coming years as one of the marvels of the ages. Who of all the officers of any State government can compare with the unassuming, dignified, and manly Oscar J. Dunn, Louisiana's first negro lieutenant-governor, or with Antoine Dubuclet, her honest and clean-handed treasurer for twelve years? His successor, E. A. Burke, a white man, representing the virtue and intelligence of our 'higher civilization,' is to-day a fugitive from the State for having robbed that same treasury of nearly a million dollars. Alabama has had her Vincent, Tennessee her Polk, Mississippi her Hemingway, Kentucky, Maryland, and nearly every one of the Southern States have had their absconding State treasurers, with hundreds of thousands of dollars of the people's money unaccounted for, since the overthrow of the negro governments of the South. Such is the contrast that I like to offer to those people who are constantly denouncing the negro governments of reconstruction times in the South.

"If our people did so well when only a few years removed from the house of bondage, wherein they were not permitted to learn to read and write under penalty of death or something next to it, what may we not expect of them with the advances they have since made and are making?"

"I declare, colonel, I would not miss this interview I have had with you for a great deal. I was so young when the war broke out that I had no personal knowledge of many of the things that you have told me, and I assure you that you have interested me with their recital. I understand that you occupied several very important positions in State affairs during the period of 'negro supremacy,' as the white people call it, and I know you must have made some valuable observations growing out of the downfall of those governments and the condition and tendencies of things since. Tell me just what you think of our future in this country, anyway. Tell me whether we are progressing or retrograding, and whether you think it is necessary for us to emigrate to Africa or to be colonized somewhere, or what?"

"Well, madam, I must confess that some of your questions are extremely hard to answer. Indeed, some of them are to-day puzzling some of the profoundest philosophers and thinkers in this country; and I doubt very much whether I could assume to answer them dogmatically. One thing, however, I can tell you without fear of successful contradiction, and that is that no people similarly situated have ever made the progress in every department of life that our people have made, since the world began. Why, just think of it! Twenty-seven years ago we did not own a foot of land, not a cottage in this wilderness, not a house, not a church, not a school-house, not even a name. We had no marriage-tie, not a legal family—nothing but the public highways, closely guarded by black laws and vagrancy laws, upon which to stand. But to-day we have two millions of our children in school, we have about eighteen thousand colored professors and teachers, twenty thousand young men and women in schools of higher grade, two hundred newspapers, over two million members in the Methodist and Baptist Churches alone, and we own over three hundred million dollars' worth of property in this Southern country. Over a million and a half of our people can now read and write. We are crowding the bar, the pulpit, and all the trades, and every avenue of civilized life, and doing credit to the age in which we live.

"I tell you, madam, I am not much disturbed about our future. True, I cannot and do not pretend to be able to solve the negro problem, as it is called, because I do not know that there is really such a problem. To my mind it is all a matter of condition and national and constitutional authority. Get the conditions right, and my faith is that the natural functions, security to 'life, liberty, and happiness,' will follow. My advice to my people is: 'Save your earnings, get homes, educate your children, build up character, obey the laws of your country, serve God, protest against injustice like manly and reasonable men, exercise every constitutional right every time you may lawfully and peacefully do so, and leave results with God, and every thing will come out right sooner or later.' I have no faith in any general emigration or colonization scheme for our people. The thing is impracticable and undesirable. This is the most beautiful and desirable country that the sun shines upon, and I am not in favor of leaving it for any place but heaven, and that when my heavenly Father calls, and not before. Of course, in localities where inhumanities are visited upon our people to such an extent that they cannot live there in peace and security I would advise them to remove to more agreeable sections of the country; but never would I advise them to leave the United States. Another thing: I do not think we ought to ever want to get into any territory to ourselves, with the white people all to one side of us or around us. That's the way they got the Indians, you remember, and we know too well what became of them.

"My plan is for us to stay right in this country with the white people, and to be so scattered in and among them that they can't hurt one of us without hurting some of their own number. That's my plan, and that is one of my reasons why I am in the Methodist Episcopal Church. God's plan seems to be to pattern this country after heaven. He is bringing here all nations, kindreds, and tongues of people and mixing them into one homogeneous whole; and I do not believe we should seek to frustrate his plan by any vain attempts to colonize ourselves in any corner to ourselves."

With this the colonel left, expressing himself delighted with his visit, as I am sure I was.

CHAPTER XIX
THE COLORED DELEGATES

The General Conference of the Methodist Episcopal Church, 1888—Negro delegates—Reception tendered them by Mrs. General Grant—Presentation of a Bible to Mrs. Grant—Dr. Minor's great presentation address.

THE following year, during the month of May, I visited the General Conference of the Methodist Episcopal Church, which was then in session in the city of New York. It was the most representative body I had ever met in my life. There were representatives there from every State and Territory in the United States, from all parts of North and South America, and from Europe, Asia, Africa, and the isles of the sea.

In that assembly were also fifty-three colored delegates, sandwiched promiscuously everywhere like so much black pepper in a vessel of salt. They took part in all the deliberations of the Conference, and were received everywhere with the utmost cordiality. Some of them acted as secretaries of the general body; others were secretaries of committees, while they were represented on all the great committees, special and standing, of that body. They were an excellent body of men, and represented their constituencies with becoming dignity and character. I really felt proud of them. But I want to tell you of an incident which took place while I was there, and to which I was permitted to be a witness.

Mrs. General U. S. Grant prepared and extended a grand reception, in her palatial mansion, to the colored delegates in the Conference. Among her invited guests, besides the delegates and such of their families and friends as accompanied them, were General John Eaton, ex-United States Commissioner of Education;

United States Senator Leland Stanford, the millionaire senator from California, and wife; Bishop and Mrs. John F. Hurst, Bishop and Mrs. John P. Newman, and other distinguished guests. Then there were also present her son, Colonel Fred. D. Grant, now United States Minister to Austria, and wife, and several of her grandchildren. The ladies here mentioned received with the Grant family. The delegates manifested their appreciation by purchasing a beautiful Bagster Bible, which was presented to Mrs. Grant as a token of their esteem. The gentleman selected to make the presentation address was introduced to Mrs. Grant and proceeded to deliver his address, to the delight of all present.

But who do you suppose he was? Why, bless you! it proved to be no other than the Rev. Dr. Daniel Minor, the son of Uncle Jacob Turner, one of Uncle Cephas's fellow-servants, who was willed free by his master, but who was sold in Tennessee at the same time that Uncle Cephas was sold. Dr. Minor was sold from his father when he was only six years old; so he was raised by his master, who gave him the name of Dan Minor. But I tell you, his speech was a real masterpiece of polished eloquence, and was delivered with such marked effect as to charm, subdue, and bring forth tears from many that stood and heard it. I know you would have been glad to have been there and to have heard it; so I shall try to repeat it for you. Said he:

"Mrs. General Grant, the colored delegates to the General Conference of the Methodist Episcopal Church, now in session in this city, in the name of the quarter of a million members which they represent, come to pay their respects to you, and to assure you of their grateful devotion and fidelity to the cherished memory of your deceased husband, and of their high appreciation of yourself and of all who were near and dear to him. We honor the illustrious names of all the great and good men and women who were instrumental in our liberation and enfranchisement in this country; but no name in American history—yes, I can safely say that no name outside of the sacred Scripture—is so dear to us as that of General Ulysses S. Grant. His name is enshrined in our memory. Lincoln's pen declared us free, but Grant's sword sundered our fetters. Israel praised God for 'the sword of the Lord and of Gideon'; we praise God for the sword of the Lord and of Grant. As a soldier he freed us; as President he protected us in our rights; and as an honored private citizen he befriended us. While he belted the earth on his foreign tour, receiving the homage of monarch and of princes, our liveliest interest and appreciation followed him to the ends of the earth. When he returned to his native land our arms and hearts were exultantly opened wide for his reception. Our admiration and joy knew no bound, and all the powers behind the throne could not resist us in our efforts to have him honored with the presidency for a third term. If his friends failed in their attempt, we have the proud satisfaction of knowing that our race never faltered in his support. . . . When General Grant visited my native State, on his return from the Orientals, I had the distinguished honor and pleasure of delivering to him an address of welcome in behalf of the colored ministers of our city, in the course of which I called his attention to an incident which had recently taken place in Florida; and I take pleasure in repeating it now to you. At a certain hotel there many of our people called to see and pay their respects to him. The proprietor of the hotel in question was offensively affected by their presence, and sought to drive them away. Did General Grant tamely submit to the harsh and inhuman treatment about to be visited upon us? No; said he, 'Let them come in, for where I am, there they may come also; if not at this, then at some other hotel.' This, to us, is one of the most precious treasures that we have inherited from him.

"During the long, weary months of his terrible affliction many sympathizing hearts with tearful eyes watched the daily bulletins giving account of his wonderful struggles between life and death. The nations had their fingers on his pulse. They counted his breathing, watched his temperature, dwelt upon every change in his diet, appetite, strength, and treatment. When the summons came, and he that had never lost a battle went down beneath the conquering hand of death, leaving your heart and home in desolation, a cry of lamentation went up throughout the land. Messages of sympathy and condolence poured in upon you from the palaces of the rich and the hovels of the poor, from every State in this country and from many of the crowned heads of other lands; but we can assure you that no hearts were more deeply wounded, no eyes wept more bitterly, and no mourners were more genuine than those of the people we represent. They, of all the people, next to yourself and immediate family, sustained the greatest loss and experienced the greatest pain.

"Our only comfort came from the knowledge that, through the blessed Gospel which we preach, he had conquered death, and from the knowledge that he had been spared to complete his great book which would make his dear family comfortable. With no mass of wealth at our command, we have not been able to embody our devotion to him in marble or in brass; but, purer and more precious and enduring than the purest marble or the costliest brass, he has, by his own deeds, established in our heart of hearts a throne of power which all the flames and floods of all the succeeding ages can never destroy or impair.

"And now, as a token of our love and eternal devotion to his sacred memory, and of our alliance to his family, we beg you to accept this token, this Holy Book, which General Grant called the sheet-anchor of our liberties; this Holy Book, which teaches us our relation to God as our Father, man as our brother, and which fits us for holy living and prepares us for happy dying. Accept it as the pledge of our devotion to his memory, to yourself, and to all your dear ones."

Now, wasn't that a grand speech? And then to think that such a man was once a poor, down-trodden slave! I tell you, there must be hope for a race that can produce such men in such a short length of time and with such limited opportunities.

Bishop Newman then responded, in behalf of the family, in a very excellent address, which all greatly enjoyed. The delegates and other invited guests were then ushered into the capacious and brilliantly lighted dining-room, where all the choicest delicacies of the season were served them by the distinguished ladies that assisted Mrs. Grant in the offices of the occasion. The many valuable and rare treasures and mementoes presented to the general by princes and potentates of foreign lands were then shown the visitors. An hour or more was spent in the most pleasant recital of reminiscences of the general's attitude toward the colored people, during and since the war, by General Eaton, Bishop Newman, and others; and the delightful and memorable affair passed into history. I need not tell you that I enjoyed the occasion. Who would not?

CHAPTER XX

A TOUCHING INCIDENT

The Cotton Centennial Exposition of 1884—Dr. Lee's great speech—
Aunt Jane Lee finds her long-lost son—The reunion.

I CANNOT close my story until I tell you of a very touching incident which I can never forget, which took place about four years before that which I have just related. I know you will enjoy it, and therefore I don't feel that it is necessary for me to make any further apology for going back to recall it. The incident took place during the great Cotton Centennial Exposition which was held in New Orleans in 1884. It was one of the finest and most extensive ever witnessed in any country. On one of the many special days that were observed there I had the pleasure of listening to many very eloquent and gifted orators, and among them was a young colored man who was said to have been a slave, and who was to speak as the representative of his race. The programme was a long and tedious one, and the people grew tired and restless; but of the sixty thousand people that had gathered nearly all remained to the last in order to get a chance to hear the colored man that would dare attempt to interest such a concourse of people after so many able orators had almost nauseated them with the choicest flower of classical oratory. At the appointed time, however, he made his appearance and was introduced. Although there were nearly sixty thousand people present when he uttered his first sentence you could almost have heard a pin drop, so intent was every one to hear what he would say. To say that he acquitted himself creditably but feebly expresses the fact. He did so well that not only the local press, but the press of the whole country, echoed his praise to the very skies. Indeed, he surprised the nation. Describing the occasion in *Harper's Magazine,* that matchless writer, Charles Dudley Warner, said:

"The colored citizens took their full share of the parade and the honors. Their societies marched with the others, and the races mingled on the grounds in unconscious equality of privileges. Speeches were made glorifying the State and its history, by able speakers, the governor among them; but it was the testimony of Democrats of undoubted Southern orthodoxy that the honors of the day were carried off by a colored clergyman, an educated man, who united eloquence with excellent good sense, and who spoke as a citizen of Louisiana, proud of his native State, dwelling with richness of allusion upon its history. It was a perfectly manly speech in the assertion of the rights and the position of his race, and it breathed throughout a spirit of good-will and amity in a common hope of progress. It was warmly applauded and accepted, so far as I heard, as a matter of course."

This colored man, I learned, was the Rev. Dr. Coleman Lee, pastor of a prominent church in Louisiana. I was so delighted with his speech, and felt so proud of him, that I forced my way through the crowd to shake his hand and to thank him, in the name of the race, for the honor he had reflected upon himself and his race. After congratulating him I said:

"Your name is Dr. Lee?"

"Yes," said he; "my father was a white man, and he would not let me be called by his name. So mother gave me her name, which was Lee, and so I have kept it right along."

"Are you a native of this State?" said I.

"O, yes," said he; "I am a native of this State, and was born right on Bayou Terre Bonne."

Said I, "Is your mother living?"

Said he, "The Lord only knows. She was sold from me when I was only four or five years old. She was sold and taken to Texas somewhere. I have advertised for her and inquired for her every-where, but have never been able to hear a word of her."

"Pray tell me, sir, what was her name?" said I.

Said he, "Her name was Jane Lee, who originally was sold to Louisiana from Virginia."

"Well, well!" thought I; and just as I was about to tell him about Aunt Charlotte, and what she told me of Aunt Jane Lee, there came a woman apparently about fifty or sixty years of age, who, upon hearing him, rushed wildly, and, throwing her arms around his neck, cried out, amid tears of great joy,

"My long-lost son, my long-lost son! my son, my son!"

Every body turned around to see what was the matter, only to unite in praise to God for the wonderful reunion that he had thus vouchsafed to this long-separated mother and son. I almost felt that I was one of the family, too, for Aunt Charlotte had told me so many things about Aunt Jane Lee; and now that I was permitted to form her acquaintance under such circumstances I could not restrain my tears nor my joy. I then took them to my house, which was only a few squares away, where I listened to them as they recited to each other the wonderful story of their lives during the years of their separation.

After spending nearly half the night with me and my family and friends who had gathered to witness this affecting scene we all united in singing, "Praise God, from whom all blessings flow," after which Dr. Lee led in prayer, and the company separated, and Dr. Lee and his mother left, with the promise that they would soon write. Dr. Lee was well situated in life. He had managed to work his way through college, had amassed a considerable amount of property, had married a very excellent wife, a former school-mate, and had one daughter; and now he was going to complete his family circle by the addition of his long-lost mother, who was going to accompany him to his comfortable and cultured home in Baton Rouge.

But when will all this scattered race be reunited that was thus most cruelly separated by our inhuman system of slavery? Never, till they gather before the throne of God, when all nations, great and small, shall then be called to their final account. Let us all thank God and rejoice that the unearthly institution has been swept away forever in a sea of blood never to rise again.

"Sound the loud timbrel o'er Egypt's dark sea;
Jehovah has triumphed, his people are free!
Sing, for the pride of this tyrant is broken,
    His chariots, his horsemen, all splendid and brave—
How void was their boast, for the Lord hath but spoken
And chariot and horsemen are sunk in the wave.
Sound the loud timbrel o'er Egypt's dark sea;
Jehovah has triumphed, his people are free!

Praise to the Conqueror, praise to the Lord!
His word was our arrow, his breath was our sword.
Who shall return to tell Egypt the story
    Of those she sent forth in the hour of her pride?
For the Lord hath looked out from his pillar of glory,
    And all the brave thousands are dashed in the tide.
Sound the loud timbrel o'er Egypt's dark sea;
Jehovah has triumphed, his people are free!"

A CATALOG OF SELECTED
DOVER BOOKS
IN ALL FIELDS OF INTEREST

A CATALOG OF SELECTED DOVER
BOOKS IN ALL FIELDS OF INTEREST

CONCERNING THE SPIRITUAL IN ART, Wassily Kandinsky. Pioneering work by father of abstract art. Thoughts on color theory, nature of art. Analysis of earlier masters. 12 illustrations. 80pp. of text. 5⅜ x 8½. 23411-8

ANIMALS: 1,419 Copyright-Free Illustrations of Mammals, Birds, Fish, Insects, etc., Jim Harter (ed.). Clear wood engravings present, in extremely lifelike poses, over 1,000 species of animals. One of the most extensive pictorial sourcebooks of its kind. Captions. Index. 284pp. 9 x 12. 23766-4

CELTIC ART: The Methods of Construction, George Bain. Simple geometric techniques for making Celtic interlacements, spirals, Kells-type initials, animals, humans, etc. Over 500 illustrations. 160pp. 9 x 12. (Available in U.S. only.) 22923-8

AN ATLAS OF ANATOMY FOR ARTISTS, Fritz Schider. Most thorough reference work on art anatomy in the world. Hundreds of illustrations, including selections from works by Vesalius, Leonardo, Goya, Ingres, Michelangelo, others. 593 illustrations. 192pp. 7⅛ x 10¼. 20241-0

CELTIC HAND STROKE-BY-STROKE (Irish Half-Uncial from "The Book of Kells"): An Arthur Baker Calligraphy Manual, Arthur Baker. Complete guide to creating each letter of the alphabet in distinctive Celtic manner. Covers hand position, strokes, pens, inks, paper, more. Illustrated. 48pp. 8¼ x 11. 24336-2

EASY ORIGAMI, John Montroll. Charming collection of 32 projects (hat, cup, pelican, piano, swan, many more) specially designed for the novice origami hobbyist. Clearly illustrated easy-to-follow instructions insure that even beginning papercrafters will achieve successful results. 48pp. 8¼ x 11. 27298-2

THE COMPLETE BOOK OF BIRDHOUSE CONSTRUCTION FOR WOODWORKERS, Scott D. Campbell. Detailed instructions, illustrations, tables. Also data on bird habitat and instinct patterns. Bibliography. 3 tables. 63 illustrations in 15 figures. 48pp. 5¼ x 8½. 24407-5

BLOOMINGDALE'S ILLUSTRATED 1886 CATALOG: Fashions, Dry Goods and Housewares, Bloomingdale Brothers. Famed merchants' extremely rare catalog depicting about 1,700 products: clothing, housewares, firearms, dry goods, jewelry, more. Invaluable for dating, identifying vintage items. Also, copyright-free graphics for artists, designers. Co-published with Henry Ford Museum & Greenfield Village. 160pp. 8¼ x 11. 25780-0

HISTORIC COSTUME IN PICTURES, Braun & Schneider. Over 1,450 costumed figures in clearly detailed engravings–from dawn of civilization to end of 19th century. Captions. Many folk costumes. 256pp. 8⅜ x 11¾. 23150-X

THE WIT AND HUMOR OF OSCAR WILDE, Alvin Redman (ed.). More than 1,000 ripostes, paradoxes, wisecracks: Work is the curse of the drinking classes; I can resist everything except temptation; etc. 258pp. 5⅜ x 8½. 20602-5

SHAKESPEARE LEXICON AND QUOTATION DICTIONARY, Alexander Schmidt. Full definitions, locations, shades of meaning in every word in plays and poems. More than 50,000 exact quotations. 1,485pp. 6½ x 9¼. 2-vol. set.
Vol. 1: 22726-X
Vol. 2: 22727-8

SELECTED POEMS, Emily Dickinson. Over 100 best-known, best-loved poems by one of America's foremost poets, reprinted from authoritative early editions. No comparable edition at this price. Index of first lines. 64pp. 5³⁄₁₆ x 8¼. 26466-1

THE INSIDIOUS DR. FU-MANCHU, Sax Rohmer. The first of the popular mystery series introduces a pair of English detectives to their archnemesis, the diabolical Dr. Fu-Manchu. Flavorful atmosphere, fast-paced action, and colorful characters enliven this classic of the genre. 208pp. 5³⁄₁₆ x 8¼. 29898-1

THE MALLEUS MALEFICARUM OF KRAMER AND SPRENGER, translated by Montague Summers. Full text of most important witchhunter's "bible," used by both Catholics and Protestants. 278pp. 6⅝ x 10. 22802-9

SPANISH STORIES/CUENTOS ESPAÑOLES: A Dual-Language Book, Angel Flores (ed.). Unique format offers 13 great stories in Spanish by Cervantes, Borges, others. Faithful English translations on facing pages. 352pp. 5⅜ x 8½. 25399-6

GARDEN CITY, LONG ISLAND, IN EARLY PHOTOGRAPHS, 1869–1919, Mildred H. Smith. Handsome treasury of 118 vintage pictures, accompanied by carefully researched captions, document the Garden City Hotel fire (1899), the Vanderbilt Cup Race (1908), the first airmail flight departing from the Nassau Boulevard Aerodrome (1911), and much more. 96pp. 8⅞ x 11¾. 40669-5

OLD QUEENS, N.Y., IN EARLY PHOTOGRAPHS, Vincent F. Seyfried and William Asadorian. Over 160 rare photographs of Maspeth, Jamaica, Jackson Heights, and other areas. Vintage views of DeWitt Clinton mansion, 1939 World's Fair and more. Captions. 192pp. 8⅞ x 11. 26358-4

CAPTURED BY THE INDIANS: 15 Firsthand Accounts, 1750-1870, Frederick Drimmer. Astounding true historical accounts of grisly torture, bloody conflicts, relentless pursuits, miraculous escapes and more, by people who lived to tell the tale. 384pp. 5⅜ x 8½. 24901-8

THE WORLD'S GREAT SPEECHES (Fourth Enlarged Edition), Lewis Copeland, Lawrence W. Lamm, and Stephen J. McKenna. Nearly 300 speeches provide public speakers with a wealth of updated quotes and inspiration–from Pericles' funeral oration and William Jennings Bryan's "Cross of Gold Speech" to Malcolm X's powerful words on the Black Revolution and Earl of Spenser's tribute to his sister, Diana, Princess of Wales. 944pp. 5⅜ x 8⅜. 40903-1

THE BOOK OF THE SWORD, Sir Richard F. Burton. Great Victorian scholar/adventurer's eloquent, erudite history of the "queen of weapons"–from prehistory to early Roman Empire. Evolution and development of early swords, variations (sabre, broadsword, cutlass, scimitar, etc.), much more. 336pp. 6⅛ x 9¼. 25434-8

AUTOBIOGRAPHY: The Story of My Experiments with Truth, Mohandas K. Gandhi. Boyhood, legal studies, purification, the growth of the Satyagraha (nonviolent protest) movement. Critical, inspiring work of the man responsible for the freedom of India. 480pp. 5⅜ x 8½. (Available in U.S. only.) 24593-4

CELTIC MYTHS AND LEGENDS, T. W. Rolleston. Masterful retelling of Irish and Welsh stories and tales. Cuchulain, King Arthur, Deirdre, the Grail, many more. First paperback edition. 58 full-page illustrations. 512pp. 5⅜ x 8½. 26507-2

THE PRINCIPLES OF PSYCHOLOGY, William James. Famous long course complete, unabridged. Stream of thought, time perception, memory, experimental methods; great work decades ahead of its time. 94 figures. 1,391pp. 5⅜ x 8½. 2-vol. set.
Vol. I: 20381-6 Vol. II: 20382-4

THE WORLD AS WILL AND REPRESENTATION, Arthur Schopenhauer. Definitive English translation of Schopenhauer's life work, correcting more than 1,000 errors, omissions in earlier translations. Translated by E. F. J. Payne. Total of 1,269pp. 5⅜ x 8½. 2-vol. set. Vol. 1: 21761-2 Vol. 2: 21762-0

MAGIC AND MYSTERY IN TIBET, Madame Alexandra David-Neel. Experiences among lamas, magicians, sages, sorcerers, Bonpa wizards. A true psychic discovery. 32 illustrations. 321pp. 5⅜ x 8½. (Available in U.S. only.) 22682-4

THE EGYPTIAN BOOK OF THE DEAD, E. A. Wallis Budge. Complete reproduction of Ani's papyrus, finest ever found. Full hieroglyphic text, interlinear transliteration, word-for-word translation, smooth translation. 533pp. 6½ x 9¼. 21866-X

MATHEMATICS FOR THE NONMATHEMATICIAN, Morris Kline. Detailed, college-level treatment of mathematics in cultural and historical context, with numerous exercises. Recommended Reading Lists. Tables. Numerous figures. 641pp. 5⅜ x 8½.
24823-2

PROBABILISTIC METHODS IN THE THEORY OF STRUCTURES, Isaac Elishakoff. Well-written introduction covers the elements of the theory of probability from two or more random variables, the reliability of such multivariable structures, the theory of random function, Monte Carlo methods of treating problems incapable of exact solution, and more. Examples. 502pp. 5⅜ x 8½. 40691-1

THE RIME OF THE ANCIENT MARINER, Gustave Doré, S. T. Coleridge. Doré's finest work; 34 plates capture moods, subtleties of poem. Flawless full-size reproductions printed on facing pages with authoritative text of poem. "Beautiful. Simply beautiful."–*Publisher's Weekly.* 77pp. 9¼ x 12. 22305-1

NORTH AMERICAN INDIAN DESIGNS FOR ARTISTS AND CRAFTSPEOPLE, Eva Wilson. Over 360 authentic copyright-free designs adapted from Navajo blankets, Hopi pottery, Sioux buffalo hides, more. Geometrics, symbolic figures, plant and animal motifs, etc. 128pp. 8⅜ x 11. (Not for sale in the United Kingdom.) 25341-4

SCULPTURE: Principles and Practice, Louis Slobodkin. Step-by-step approach to clay, plaster, metals, stone; classical and modern. 253 drawings, photos. 255pp. 8⅛ x 11.
22960-2

THE INFLUENCE OF SEA POWER UPON HISTORY, 1660–1783, A. T. Mahan. Influential classic of naval history and tactics still used as text in war colleges. First paperback edition. 4 maps. 24 battle plans. 640pp. 5⅜ x 8½. 25509-3

CATALOG OF DOVER BOOKS

THE STORY OF THE TITANIC AS TOLD BY ITS SURVIVORS, Jack Winocour (ed.). What it was really like. Panic, despair, shocking inefficiency, and a little heroism. More thrilling than any fictional account. 26 illustrations. 320pp. 5⅜ x 8½.
20610-6

FAIRY AND FOLK TALES OF THE IRISH PEASANTRY, William Butler Yeats (ed.). Treasury of 64 tales from the twilight world of Celtic myth and legend: "The Soul Cages," "The Kildare Pooka," "King O'Toole and his Goose," many more. Introduction and Notes by W. B. Yeats. 352pp. 5⅜ x 8½.
26941-8

BUDDHIST MAHAYANA TEXTS, E. B. Cowell and others (eds.). Superb, accurate translations of basic documents in Mahayana Buddhism, highly important in history of religions. The Buddha-karita of Asvaghosha, Larger Sukhavativyuha, more. 448pp. 5⅜ x 8½.
25552-2

ONE TWO THREE . . . INFINITY: Facts and Speculations of Science, George Gamow. Great physicist's fascinating, readable overview of contemporary science: number theory, relativity, fourth dimension, entropy, genes, atomic structure, much more. 128 illustrations. Index. 352pp. 5⅜ x 8½.
25664-2

EXPERIMENTATION AND MEASUREMENT, W. J. Youden. Introductory manual explains laws of measurement in simple terms and offers tips for achieving accuracy and minimizing errors. Mathematics of measurement, use of instruments, experimenting with machines. 1994 edition. Foreword. Preface. Introduction. Epilogue. Selected Readings. Glossary. Index. Tables and figures. 128pp. 5⅜ x 8½.
40451-X

DALÍ ON MODERN ART: The Cuckolds of Antiquated Modern Art, Salvador Dalí. Influential painter skewers modern art and its practitioners. Outrageous evaluations of Picasso, Cézanne, Turner, more. 15 renderings of paintings discussed. 44 calligraphic decorations by Dalí. 96pp. 5⅜ x 8½. (Available in U.S. only.)
29220-7

ANTIQUE PLAYING CARDS: A Pictorial History, Henry René D'Allemagne. Over 900 elaborate, decorative images from rare playing cards (14th–20th centuries): Bacchus, death, dancing dogs, hunting scenes, royal coats of arms, players cheating, much more. 96pp. 9¼ x 12¼.
29265-7

MAKING FURNITURE MASTERPIECES: 30 Projects with Measured Drawings, Franklin H. Gottshall. Step-by-step instructions, illustrations for constructing handsome, useful pieces, among them a Sheraton desk, Chippendale chair, Spanish desk, Queen Anne table and a William and Mary dressing mirror. 224pp. 8⅛ x 11¼.
29338-6

THE FOSSIL BOOK: A Record of Prehistoric Life, Patricia V. Rich et al. Profusely illustrated definitive guide covers everything from single-celled organisms and dinosaurs to birds and mammals and the interplay between climate and man. Over 1,500 illustrations. 760pp. 7½ x 10⅛.
29371-8